BMW
M-SERIES AND
PERFORMANCE SPECIALS

Jonathan Cohen

Motorbooks International
Publishers & Wholesalers ®

Dedication
To Jennifer and Benjamin

First published in 1996 by Motorbooks International Publishers & Wholesalers, 729 Prospect Avenue, PO Box 1, Osceola WI 54020 USA

Printed in Hong Kong

Library of Congress Cataloging-in-Publication Data
Cohen, Jonathan H.
BMW M–Series & performance specials / Jonathan H. Cohen.
p. cm. — (Motorbooks International sports car color history series)
ISBN 0-7603-0171-9
1. BMW automobile—History. I. Title. II. Series: Sports car color history.
TL215.B25C63 1996
629.222'2—dc20 96-9392

On the front cover: Pictured are a 1987 M3 Evolution and a 1973 3.0 CSi owned by BMW Mobile Tradition. This shot was taken in the rural countryside, just outside of Munich, Germany. *David Gooley*

On the frontispiece: Visible here is the Kevlar center console with Schnitzer's special switch panel, the Kevlar radio cover, the suede covered sports steering wheels, the aluminum pedal assembly and the specially modified analog/digital dashboard display.

On the title page: With an additional 50bhp (now up to 372bhp), and with a completely reworked suspension system, the 850CSi was significantly faster and better-handling than the standard car.

On the back cover: BMW's U.S. replacement for the M5, the 540i Sport combined the M5's suspension brakes, wheels and bodywork with the company's 4.0-liter V-8 engine. Vittorio Brambilla drives the Schnitzer 3.0CS on the Nurburgring. The BMW 4-cylinder engine lineup. From left to right; the street, Formula 2, and Formula 1 versions—all based upon the same basic design and engine block.

Contents

CHAPTER 1   **Introduction**   7

CHAPTER 2   **The Tuning Triumvirate:**
Alpina, Hartage and Schnitzer   15

CHAPTER 3   **Early High-Performance Efforts:**
The Four-Cylinder Cars   29

CHAPTER 4   **The Move Upmarket:**
High-Performance Early 6-Cylinder
Sedans and Coupes   41

CHAPTER 5   **Forging a Separate Path:**
The M1 (E-26)   49

CHAPTER 6   **The 5-Series Sedans (E-12, E-28 and E-34)**   57

CHAPTER 7   **The 3-Series Cars:**
High-Performance in a Small Package   77

CHAPTER 8   **The 6-Series Coupes**   103

CHAPTER 9   **The High-Performance 7-Series Cars**   111

CHAPTER 10   **The 8-Series Cars**   121

CHAPTER 11   **Epilogue**   127

   Index   128

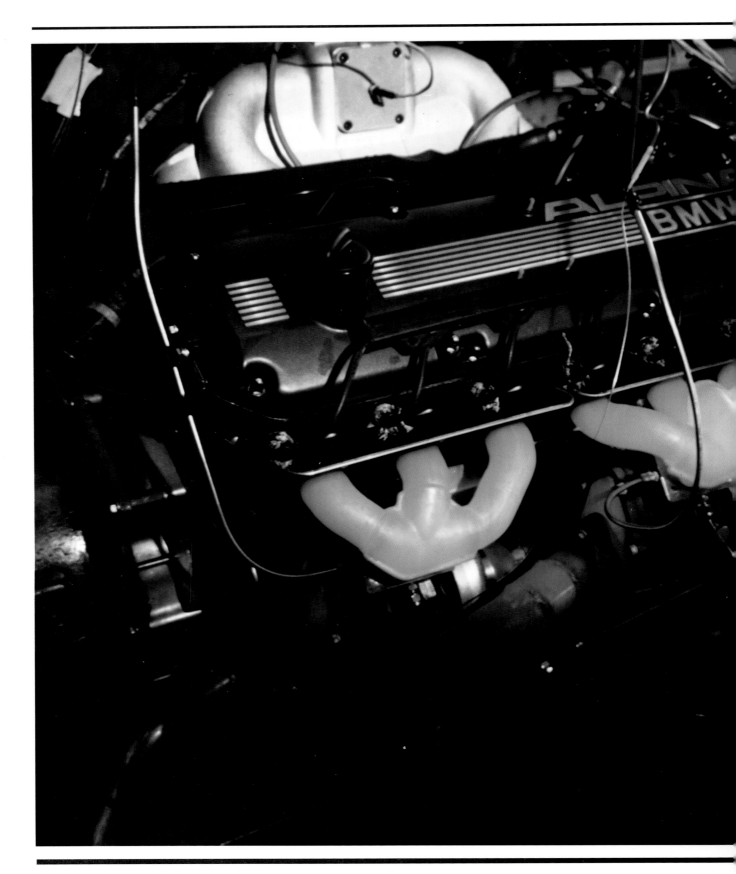

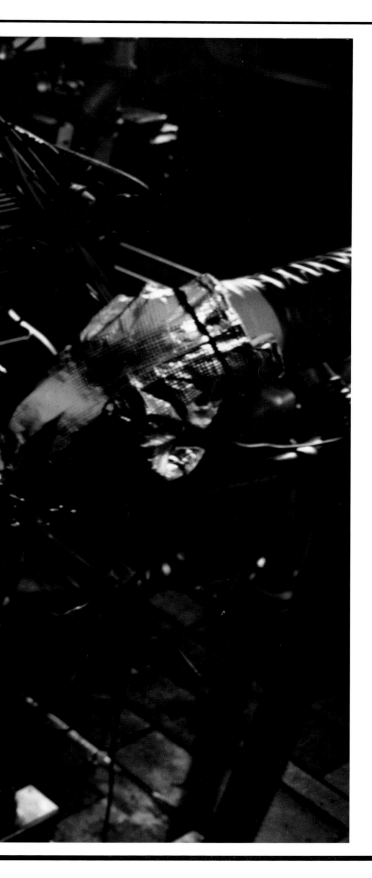

CHAPTER 1

Introduction

It must be readily evident to almost anyone who has lived in a place where there are cars, that the role of the automobile has been universally elevated beyond its nominal transportation value. Especially in the United States and in Europe, automotive enthusiasm can take any of a vast number of forms, each supported and reinforced by the automotive literature and by other people with similar interests.

If one make of automobile can move people and their belongings just as effectively as another, why should there exist such emotion attached to the choice of which automobile to own? In several parts of the world, many people spend a huge part of their income to drive a particular type of car. People who have no need for even one car own many, while entire volumes (such as this) are written extolling the virtues of one make over another.

Even against such arguments, automotive enthusiasm continues to thrive. The automobile maintains a persistent hold upon the appetites of consumers and the affections of owners. If the reason why certain automobiles inspire a passion which exceeds any rational justification is difficult to understand, than it is at least comforting to know that the question has been fully examined by at least one company. In the 1993 BMW Annual Report (a document which devotes a considerable

Exhaust manifolds glowing orange—the B10 Bi-Turbo on Alpina's test bed.

number of pages to the history of Man's time on Earth), the company notes:

> *Movement is a principle of life. In the animal kingdom, movement, and its constant improvement, is one of the most successful strategies of evolution. Study of nature teaches us there are no final solutions, only temporary ones. This also applies to the cultural version of the phenomenon, to mobility. History provides us, time and again, with new answers to the question of the best system of transport. No scientific discipline alone can reach a comprehensive conclusion. Intellectual mobility is required.*

The particular and sustained appeal of the automobile derives perhaps from two separate requirements: the basic need for transportation and the importance of manufactured objects as representations of our own abilities. BMW, perhaps better than any other company, seems acutely aware of and sensitive to these connected desires. The company believes that "civilization lives by manufactured products. They are designed for man. The designer is called upon, and undertakes, to determine the practical and emotional needs of the user. Design gives function to its form. If the design is a success, the objects are unique."(BMW Annual Report, 1992)

There must certainly exist some relationship between the consequence of the task a tool is put to and the satisfaction gained from using it effectively. Under almost any driving condition, the importance of superior equipment is immediately apparent. In the post-war period, BMW has populated the world's roads with consistently well-engineered, carefully manufactured machines. During that time, the company has built a reputation perhaps unequaled among high-volume manufacturers (which BMW now certainly is). While all of the company's cars have been of very high quality, and while many have been highly desirable, only a few have stood apart as truly high-performance vehicles. This is a history of BMW's special efforts—their highest-performance road cars. Despite their relatively small numbers, these machines have been critical in building the company's performance image, its market position and its current success.

If a common thread exists between BMW's dramatic post-war corporate recovery and the company's sustained financial strength (on a fairly massive scale), then that thread extends from the nature of the cars themselves. Despite enormous differences in their conception and purpose, all post-war BMWs have been built upon certain common principles; impeccable design and build quality have invariably been combined with qualities of lightness and maneuverability generally unavailable elsewhere.

BMW is an enterprise with a defining mission: to produce vehicles which are both dynamically superior to their competition and consistent with the needs of a broad customer base—cars which can both inspire and transport. Creating exciting vehicles is not very difficult for a small company with that as their primary objective. To produce remarkable cars while at the same time supporting the activities of a vast commercial enterprise with millions of customers worldwide is a very different assignment. BMW, largely because of their basic philosophy and perhaps alone among all automotive companies, has consistently managed to reconcile these two ambitions. While many other companies have offered blistering fast cars of no real usefulness, BMW has always built cars of immense practicality with a generally high level of performance. For those who have wanted even higher levels of performance, that too has been available. I believe that the cars presented here represent the purest manifestation of the company's mission. Both physically and emotionally, they continue to move their owners.

HIGH PERFORMANCE IN A PRACTICAL PACKAGE

Historically, the great majority of the world's manufacturers of very high performance automobiles have been generally unconcerned with issues such as comfort, durability, fuel economy or luggage space. Just as fashionable clothes are meant to be worn for a short while and then discarded for the next season's collection, most of the world's highest performance sports cars were never intended to provide the basis for a long-term relationship. This thinking is perhaps most evident to owners of even relatively young, low-mileage exotic cars, who are surprised at the need for complete and expensive restoration.

As a producer of millions of automobiles annually, BMW cannot afford to indulge in that sort of thinking. Unlike the products of smaller companies with less at stake, BMWs are carefully engineered and robustly constructed according to the needs of their customers. While most BMWs are capable of strong performance, they must also be capable of carrying their owners comfortably and quietly.

If nothing else, and even if price is not an issue, then building a high-performance automobile on a reasonably practical platform means that the car will be used much more frequently. Exotic two-seat automobiles are not generally used as everyday transportation.

During the post-war period, BMW has occupied a unique niche in the market for quality-built cars. More involving to drive, and with better performance than competing models from Mercedes (and better-built than almost anything else), BMW created the term "sports-sedan" and continues to provide reference-standard products within that category.

At the corporate level, no other manufacturer, even a fraction BMW's size, has been as consistently dedicated to the production of high performance vehicles. If the cars presented here are unlike any others, it is because they have been created to be used as serious transportation by a company committed to that purpose on a huge scale. If they are significantly more interesting than the output of other industrial concerns operating on a similar scale, it is because BMW has and continues to see themselves as a company with a clearly defined purpose.

> *Without mobility, most people would be unable to do their work, take care of themselves, or get to know other people and cultures. Indeed, they would even be denied training, education and many other amenities of life.*
> —BMW Annual Report, 1992

Despite the enthusiasm which goes into their design and construction, every BMW represents some compromise between dynamic performance and factors such as comfort, longevity and efficiency. Because the cars have historically attracted enthusiastic owners, and because of the strength of the basic platform, BMWs have always encouraged modifications. Given that there exist only a relatively few legitimately special BMWs, and in view of the enormous number of cars which have been in some way modified to imitate higher-performance versions, it is important to differentiate between the two groups. While there exists no reason why an enthusiastic owner or tuning firm should not feel free to alter their car, there is no doubt that details of original, factory-level performance efforts have been obscured by this process. The performance tuning products of BMW (through their Motorsports division) and Alpina are considered more desirable because of their integration with the factory's ongoing product development efforts.

DIFFERENTIATING BETWEEN FACTORY, ORIGINAL AND AFTERMARKET

Perhaps the most difficult part of any analysis of limited-production automobiles is in differentiating between factory vehicles and the efforts of aftermarket companies or enthusiastic owners. In view of the large supply of aftermarket BMW equipment, and given the historic eagerness of BMW owners to modify their cars, this issue becomes especially important here.

For the purpose of this work, we have segmented those vehicles under discussion into three primary groups;

1) Cars which originally left the factory (BMW's, BMW Motorsport's or Alpina's) in their final form. This includes all the production Motorsport cars, factory/Motorsport specials and those Alpina cars which were actually built by Alpina (meaning those cars which were supplied new by that company and typically provided with Alpina serial numbers). While subsequent changes to these vehicles may not diminish their appeal or desirability, cars which began as normal production vehicles and were modified later in life would not fall into this category.

2) Vehicles which were sympathetically modified in accordance with programs designed by BMW Motorsport, Alpina, Hartage or Schnitzer (possibly by those companies themselves), after being used in their original form. Many of the most interesting special BMWs throughout the world (and especially in the U.S.) fall into this category. We would include here essentially all of the cars modified by companies such as Hardy & Beck and Miller and Norburn as U.S. Alpina cars. Also included are those older cars which have been built as Motorsport or Alpina replicas using original (and now very difficult to obtain) parts. Many of these cars are enormously interesting, and, in the case of certain older cars modified early in their

life, of potentially greater historical interest than some cars in the first category.

3) The third category includes those cars which have been modified without significant regard to historical precedent or authenticity. Most modified BMWs fall into this category; however they are the least interested for the purposes of this work.

THE SECONDARY MARKET;
VALUE VS. WORTH

At present there exists only a coarse relationship between the historical significance or mechanical virtue of certain cars and their price as determined by the market. While we will not ascribe specific price values to the cars discussed here (prices which would be quickly outdated), we will attempt to allot some subjective measure of worth to these vehicles.

If there can be no practical distinction drawn between an original road-going product of BMW's Motorsport division and a carefully constructed replica, why then should there exist an enormous and persistent disparity between their market values (this distinction also holds true for Alpina cars)? The answer must relate to the idea of originality in determining the value of any artifact. Just as a reproduction of a historically important painting or statue may be valued for its aesthetics, the original will be much more highly valued for its historic significance. While it is doubtful that any of the creations of industrial production should ever be elevated to the status of renowned art, certain of these products reflect the creativity and abilities of their makers with a clarity equal to any of the products of the fine arts.

The cars presented here represent a catalog of BMW's best post-war work. While owners of more ordinary examples of the company's cars may not immediately see the relationship between their cars and those presented here, the ties are in fact very strong. Many of the BMWs featured in this book have served as the models for later production cars. In some cases (such as with the Alpina 2-Liter 1600, the original 3.0CSL and the early 3.5-Liter 5-Series), cars which were created as high-performance specials—and which were seen as quite exotic at the time—actually evolved into regular factory production models.

WHY NOT MUCH THUS FAR

While almost every nation seems to produce automotive enthusiasts (even in conditions where cars are essentially unavailable), it seems that the British and the Americans have bred a disproportional high number. While the analysis necessary for a complete discussion of this condition is perhaps beyond the scope of this work, we can safely speculate that the continuing role of the automobile in American culture continues to leave a lasting impression on successive generations of enthusiasts. In England, as perhaps in no other place, the importance of a person's hobby has been elevated to the status of serious business.

Just as many of the best automotive histories tend to be English-language, so do the best English-language works tend to be about either English or American cars (although Italian cars have also received enormous English-language interest). For whatever the reason, German cars have not enjoyed the depth of English-language coverage which some feel they deserve. Thus, while there currently exists a wealth of information covering virtually every detail of most even moderately-interesting 1960s American muscle-car (some of which may be fully deserving of such attention), very little attention has been paid to conceptually similar cars from Germany.

Especially with regard to the products of the German tuners (such as Alpina), there has been notably little English-language analysis. The reason for this may relate not to any lack of enthusiasm for these cars, but rather to the fact that their export to the U.S. has been virtually nonexistent. Additionally, the U.K. has historically been deprived of many of Alpina's most interesting efforts; for example, neither the 5-series nor 6-series versions of the incredible B7 Turbo could be made in right hand-drive versions.

THE RELATIONSHIP BETWEEN
BMW'S COMPETITION AND ROAD CARS

Perhaps more so than any other automaker, BMW has consistently placed their products in direct sporting competition with other makers; the company has always raced their cars. While this work is intended as an analysis of BMW's most interesting *road* cars, it would be impossible to fully explore those vehicles without reference to the company's competition cars.

BMW emerged from World War II with little thought of motorsport competition. Survival, rather than conquest, was foremost on the company's mind. Towards that end, BMW's initial post-war offerings were geared toward earning enough cash to sustain the company's basic operations.

Especially through the 1960s to mid-1970s, the line between BMW's competitive efforts and the company's special high-performance road cars must be seen as paper-thin. While their earliest efforts at higher performance were made to produce more competitive cars for racing, BMW puts far more of what they develop on the track back into their production cars than other manufacturers.

In the factory's own words in 1979:

> *To the engineers at the Bavarian Motor Works, racing is not merely sport. Not simply a way to accumulate trophies, prizes and glory, though all of these have been earned by BMW in prodigious quantities.*
>
> *It is seen instead as a test. A yardstick by which the ability of the engineers to solve the most demanding technological and organizational problems can be measured. A proof of competence, to ourselves and to others.*
>
> *Can this not be achieved equally well on the test track or in a controlled laboratory experiment?*
>
> *To be blunt, no.*
>
> *From the non-competitive vacuum of the test track and the laboratory come cars that are predictably non-competitive.*
>
> *In racing, cars are prepared before a race - and kept going during a race - in unusual and often unfavorable conditions. And from this energy-charged situation - one that demands the greatest individual and team skills and enthusiasm - come answers to engineering questions that could not be solved in a normal working life.*
>
> *At BMW, we truly believe the result of non-participation in automotive racing is automotive mediocrity.*

Recently BMW ran advertising for the 850i with the logo: "IF A COMPANY CAN HAVE A SOUL, THIS IS OURS." In a very real sense, and consistently for the last 50 years, the company's competition efforts have defined both its spirit and its products.

THE U.S. GREY MARKET: THE AGONY AND THE ECSTACY

From the mid-1970s to mid-1980s, U.S. BMW enthusiasts were both elated and frustrated by the existence of European market-only high-performance BMWs. While the U.S. 3-, 5-, 6- and 7-series cars which made up the company's line during those years were, in many ways, meaningfully superior to the offerings of almost any other car company, they were nonetheless inferior (from an enthusiast's point of view) to models available only in Europe.

Although the E-12 5-Series (the 530i of 1976-1979 and the 528i of 1979-1981), and the E-23 7-Series (the 733i and the 735i) were both especially successful creations in their U.S.-legal versions, the E-21 3-series (320i) and the E-24 6-series (the 630CSi and 633CSi) suffered more noticeably when compared with their Rest of World (RoW) equivalents.

The existence of European market-only cars such as the early (1979-1981) 635CSi, the 745i and the first-generation 323i created a significant demand for private U.S. importation. European-specification BMWs brought into the U.S. presented American enthusiasts with a two-edged sword. Grey market cars were required to be brought into compliance with all applicable U.S. EPA and DOT regulations. A cottage industry sprang up almost immediately to perform the necessary work. Unfortunately, the quality of service offered by those companies was often lacking. Many cars which were privately imported failed to live up to the expectations of their owners or required additional work to make them usable.

For U.S. enthusiasts seeking a special high-performance BMW, that car will more often than not have been privately imported. Beyond the normal investigation into the vehicle's condition which should be performed prior to the purchase of any used car, potential buyers should ensure that the car they locate is supplied with the necessary EPA and DOT paperwork. The absence of those documents could make registration of the vehicle very difficult, if not impossible.

While this book has been written in English (and in the U.S.), it is assumed that the audience for high-performance BMWs is worldwide. As such, we have attempted to describe vehicles of interest to BMW enthusiasts regardless of location. Nonetheless, national import and export restrictions mean that some of these cars will not be available in certain areas. Especially in the case of very rare cars, we have tried to give at least some indication of where they are likely to be found.

In terms of current U.S. availability of European-specification BMWs, the outlook is relatively bleak. The very much more stringent import requirement imposed in 1968 essentially means that only those post-1967 cars already in the U.S. will likely ever be obtainable here. While there does not seem much chance for a near-term rush on European-specification 635CSis or 735is (of which there is a more than adequate supply, those cars typically trading at a meaningful discount to their U.S.-specification equivalents), it is likely that, due to their scarcity, U.S.-located Motorsport cars, M1s and Alpinas could command substantial premiums to their European market prices.

BMW: THE FACTORY SPECIALS

For most of BMW's post-war history, there have been individual customers who would have liked to own cars with higher levels of performance or fitted to a more expensive specification. While the company has historically been unwilling to indulge the desires of those individual customers (like some smaller manufactures), such cars *have* been built by the factory. These are perhaps the most interesting special BMWs, and were never considered production cars. Factory specials were typically produced on an individual basis for the company's high-level executives or for factory racing drivers; the fortunate few who were able to create unique road-going BMWs for their personal use.

Although the general public has generally been denied access to the factory's special efforts, and while very little (if any) information was ever made available by the factory, some of these cars have formed the basis for later production vehicles. An attempt to present as complete as possible an accounting of these cars has been made, but the list is far from complete.

It is important to note that, with regard to the company's primary business (large-scale road car production), these special vehicles have had an impact far greater than their very limited numbers would suggest. Many of the most popular BMW road cars have derived directly from the company's specials. Moreover, the existence of these cars (together with the products of the tuning companies), has added significantly to the reputation which BMW now enjoys.

1973 3.0 CSi owned by BMW Mobile Tradition, the company's rolling museum. *David Gooley*

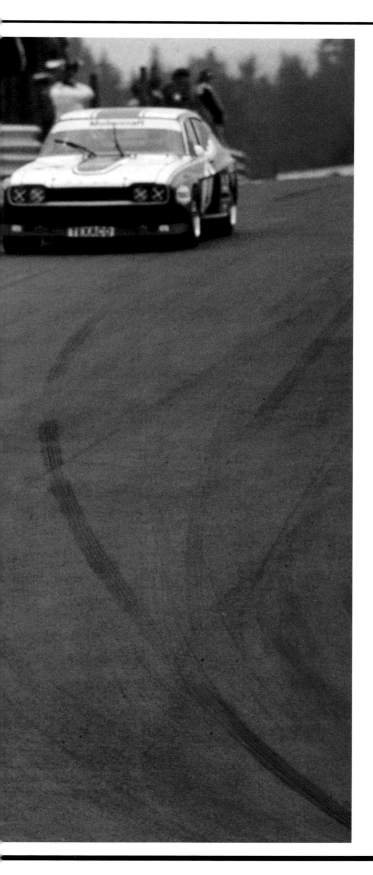

CHAPTER 2

The Tuning Triumvirate:
Alpina, Hartage and Schnitzer

Within Germany, the tradition of modifying or "tuning" standard production cars for higher levels of performance is one with a long and successful history. While this work, (performed with varying levels of professionalism and competence), is commonplace throughout the world, it has become more established as a formal business in Germany than anywhere else.

All of the BMW tuning firms discussed here have their roots firmly planted in motorsport. Beginning in the mid-1960s, the focus for each was primarily on preparing cars for competition. Out of that work and following their successes on the track, the natural progression was to sell competition-proven parts for use on road cars. With little government regulation to contend with, adapting those parts for street use was both effective and legal. These early cars used relatively straightforward tuning methods; higher compression ratios, more aggressively profiled camshafts, larger and dual-carburetion systems and firmer suspensions were all well-understood technologies by the mid-1960s.

What must be considered, especially as related to any discussion of the tuning companies' early activities, is that their work was conducted on a much less formal basis than would be the case today. In the early to mid-1960s (even in Germany), the business of racing production cars and selling

Vittorio Brambilla driving the Schnitzer 3.0CS on the Nurburgring.

components based on those race cars could be handled without the need for much bureaucracy. Indeed, conversations with those at the top of the tuning world today indicate that at the time, their work was seen more as a hobby than as a business. Maintaining records or archives was certainly not a high priority. As such, the information presented here regarding those early activities, while as complete and accurate as possible, may not fully represent all of what was happening in the world of BMW high-performance.

THE ALPINA CARS

ALPINA: "PERFORMANCE WITHOUT ALL THE PERFORMANCE"

In the minds of BMW enthusiasts, Alpina is the tuning firm most closely associated with the company. Alpina has built their business entirely upon BMW's products, and at the same time has added considerably to the larger company's image and reputation.

BMW's efforts at high-performance product development have also benefited from Alpina's activities. While the two companies have no formal corporate relationship (in terms of cross-ownership), they maintain a long-standing and mutually beneficial association. For many years, Alpina's products have built upon the basic validity of the BMW product, but have gone further in terms of performance (and cost) then BMW could themselves justify.

For the purpose of this work, Alpina is seen as essentially separate from all other BMW tuning firms. Clearly, the company's relationship with BMW goes beyond that enjoyed by any other concern, and Alpina's products are widely considered the most desirable of all specially-prepared BMWs.

ALPINA; AUTHENTICITY AND MODIFICATION

There are essentially only two categories of Alpina vehicles; those cars which were built by Alpina themselves (and which were sold new as Alpinas), and those cars modified by others using Alpina components. Differentiating between these two groups may seem relatively unimportant; in fact, the difference is critical. Of the great many BMWs modified using Alpina components, perhaps only one in a thousand (if that many) was actually prepared *by Alpina*.

Original Alpina-modified cars are complete automobiles; they were each developed and produced according to a specific and comprehensive design. Most importantly, these are *balanced* vehicles; unlike a great many pretenders, Alpina does not make modifications without consideration of their consequences—if horsepower is added, so are better suspensions and breaking systems. Nor does the company make changes for appearance alone; aerodynamic appendages improve airflow, wider wheels and tires improve roadholding and interior modifications allow the driver to control the vehicle with greater comfort and precision.

THE ALPINA STORY

Note: The following section has been taken largely from material translated directly from the Alpina archives, supplemented by the author's own research. We note that this section omits mention of many specific Alpina models. While that information is provided in the section on the individual cars, and while this history is not intended as a complete account of the Alpina company, it may provide some insight into that company's view of their accomplishments.

THE BEGINNINGS

The development of new technologies frequently produces unexpected results; the outcome of some early efforts at performance tuning in Germany would have certainly been difficult to predict.

Born in 1936, Burkhard Bovensipen founded and is still today CEO of a worldwide tuning operation built on improving BMW automobiles. It began with his purchase of a used Fiat 1500. Bovensipen brought the car over to a friend to clean up the engine compartment, give it a tune-up and to make sure it was running correctly. Rather then stop there, the two added a Weber two-barrel carburetor, a more aggressive camshaft and opened up the muffler; thus raising horsepower from 67bhp to about 75bhp. Shortly thereafter, a cloud of blue smoke began to follow the car on the autostrada—proof that the modifications were more than the Fiat's little three-main-bearing engine could handle. At that point, the two concluded that small engines were perhaps left unmodified.

Bovensipen was not to refrain from that activity for long, due largely to his interest in the cars being built by the BMW factory. At the international automobile show in 1961, the diminutive four cylinder BMW 1500 was introduced. With that introduction, the foundation was laid for the recreation of the BMW product line (vitally important, given that the range then consisted of the tiny underpowered ISETTA and the expensive and difficult-to-sell eight cylinder cars). While the new 1500 was not an inexpensive car, it was nonetheless very well received. In effect, the car addressed two markets; while the press termed it a sportscar, most customers were inclined to use the 1500 as a family vehicle. With the high revving 80bhp engine originally fitted, the 1500 was perhaps under-engined for that role.

BMW reacted quickly to the new car's apparent deficiency. At the 1963 international automobile show, the company introduced a 90 horsepower 1800cc derivation of the 1500. With the introduction of the new car, those customers who had recently purchased 1500s were understandably disappointed. Bovensipen, who was quick to recognize the considerable development potential of the BMW four cylinder engine, saw an opportunity. With four well-designed intake ports and only one (small) factory-installed carburetor, Bovensipen recognized that he could significantly improve the car's performance with modification to its intake system. With that realization, the first BMW-Alpina tuning kit was created. The kit consisted of two Webber two-barrel side draft carburetors on short intake manifolds and a large oil-bathed air filter. Financial assistance from Bovensipen's father (who owned a small mechanical parts manufacturing firm, also called Alpina) helped enormously in the production of those first tuning kits. Selling for DM 980 (including installation), Alpina's tuning kits for the 1500 raised that car's performance to parity with the newer 1800.

The first Alpina product won tacit approval from BMW themselves; after testing the kit, BMW's R&D Department could find nothing to fault with Alpina's work. Support from the factory (including BMW's sales manager Paul Hahnemann) was invaluable to Alpina. That support not only made the company's products more desirable to BMW enthusiasts, but also meant that installation of an Alpina system did not void the BMW warranty.

Bovensipen's new company did not receive immediate acclaim from the motoring press. Particularly skeptical was Gert Hack of *Auto Motor und*

Sport of Stuttgart. Mr. Hack suggested that Alpina's engine modifications would have a detrimental effect on longevity and reliability. He suggested that Bovensipen's modifications were ill-conceived, given how close BMW had come to perfection right off the production line. At the time, Mr. Hack could not have known that he would someday become a partner in the Alpina factory in Buchloe.

Bovensipen showed considerable resolve in getting Mr. Hack to actually test the car, rather then just commenting on the concept of BMW tuning. That test showed the Alpina-modified 1500 to be fully the equal of the newer 1800 model in terms of performance. The Alpina car showed no signs of stress or fragility, turning in an acceleration figure of 13.1 seconds from 0-100 kilometers per hour (62 miles per hour), and recording a top speed of 160 kilometers per hour. At the time, those figures were extremely impressive for a smaller car; the very much more expensive Mercedes Benz 220 SE (equipped with a fuel-injected 2.2 liter six cylinder engine) reached a top speed of about 170 kilometers per hour (106 miles per hour). *Auto Motor und Sport* were clearly enthusiastic about the Alpina's performance. Hack also noted that the quality of the car's fit and finish was such that it appeared to have come directly from BMW. BMW themselves were impressed; when the higher-performance 110bhp 1800 TI was introduced, it was fitted with engine components identical to those developed by Alpina. Clearly, Alpina benefited considerably from their relationship with the factory, and from the favorable publicity which resulted.

For the newly-formed tuning company, a print-based advertising campaign was not within their means. To generate interest in Alpina's products, Bovensipen distributed flyers at the Frankfurt International Auto Show, placing them under the windshield wipers of every BMW 1500. One of the slogans used in the flyers was "Aus Freude Am Fahren," which translates as "The Fun of Driving." Due in part to Alpina's efforts, BMWs began to enjoy a more sporting image; many BMW customers were happy to spend extra money to make their cars just as fast (or faster) then the current Mercedes-Benz and Porsches. At the time (the mid-1960s), bolt-on performance from Alpina was considerably less expensive then buying a new BMW

1800 TI or almost any competitors' sports cars. Among the Germany manufactures, only three models provided more horsepower than the Alpina; the Mercedes Benz 300SE, the newly-released Porsche 911, and the (completely different) Mercedes Benz 600 limousine.

With BMW's introduction of the new two-door 1600, the stage was set for the continuation of Alpina's work. The 1600 was smaller and lighter then the 1500/1800 cars, with a highly favorable power-to-weight ratio. Together with subsequent versions of the car (including the 2002 and 2002 TI), BMW essentially launched a new category—the sports sedan. These cars were configured to provide adequate room for passengers and their luggage, but were clearly built for people who were able to spend a bit more money, and who wanted a more sporting product. To those customers, the performance characteristics of their sedan were more important than a plush interior or a soft suspension. BMW owners soon found out that they could mix it up with much larger and more powerful cars on the autobahn. Alpina responded to this new and larger market with a more complete product line; now, rather then just carburetor kits, complete high-performance engines were available to the public. These engines were fitted with special lighter pistons, carefully balanced crankshafts and polished connecting rods.

When the 165bhp Alpina 2002 was tested by motoring journalist Paul Frere for the Belgian magazine *Sport Moteur*, he wrote that "On my test runs at the Vallelunga Race Track, the Alpina BMW ran an amazingly fast time of 1:04 minutes. That time was one second faster then that recorded by the Lamborghini Miura and 5.1 seconds better then the record holder from two years before, the Porsche 911S. Given its high level of tune, the Alpina motor displayed an enormous level of flexibility." Mr. Frere went on to comment that, apart from its pure performance potential, the Alpina BMW made a wonderful grand tourer.

By the late 1960s and early 1970s, Bovensiepen and Alpina had established an international reputation for their performance conversions. The company's status went a long way towards changing the common perception of high-performance aftermarket tuners; that they were generally incompetents who built engines which made considerable power for only a very short time. With Alpina, legitimate science and engineering were applied to the problem of making more power while retaining driveability and longevity.

With the success of Alpina's performance accessories business, the company moved towards building and selling complete Alpina-modified BMWs. These cars offered a range of different horsepower engines, along with complete suspension packages and a wide range of special ancillary components. What differentiated Alpina from other tuners was their ability to create a *complete* performance car; the company began to go so far as to custom manufacture parts such as A-arms, shock absorbers and brake components to fit their own requirements. Alpina also began to offer the option of a complete special interior package to complement their modified cars. The company's objective had clearly shifted; rather then selling high-performance packages, Alpina now offered complete high-quality automobiles with the emphasis on usable performance. While the company's cars were (and remain) expensive, the price is more easily understood when their careful engineering and very high levels of quality are taken into account.

In addition to their BMW conversions for the road, Alpina added to their growing international reputation through competition. All of the company's work continued to be undertaken in the City of Buchloe—adding to the that city's economy. By 1970, Alpina BMW's had won the Tour De Europe, 24-hour races in Spain and France and most rallies held in Germany. Most German hill climbs were won by BMWs with the Alpina name across their sides. Between 1964 and 1973, the list of drivers who competed in Alpina-modified BMW's read like a who's who of the racing world. Those drivers included Jacky Ickx, James Hunt, Hans Stuck, Derek Bell, Harold Ertle, Brian Muir, and the world famous Nicki Lauda. These drivers distinguished not only themselves, but also the Alpina-modified BMWs in which they competed. By the early-1970s, the name BMW-Alpina had become widely-recognized. For both BMW and Alpina, the relationship was an enormous and ongoing success; Alpina availed themselves of BMW's products and engineering, while BMW derived considerable glory from Alpina's competition activities. Although Alpina was nominally treated as any other good customer (the company now purchased approximately 500 new BMWs annually for modification), the relationship had moved forward, towards the sharing of resources and talent.

AN IDEAL BASE

While the desire to own a unique automobile is shared by many drivers, the vast majority reconcile themselves to the manufacturers' standard offerings. By the early-1970s, BMW enthusiasts had a legitimate alternative to driving a standard BMW. What had become clear (largely through Alpina's efforts) was that even a highly-developed car could be made to produce more power. While BMWs of the period were more highly tuned then most of their competitors, there was nonetheless still room for improvement. Where Alpina excelled was not in terms of mass produced quality, but rather through careful reworking of specific components to a standard which would not have been feasible for the BMW factory. Alpina engines were superior to standard BMW engines not because Alpina engineers were necessarily more skilled, but rather because they (and their customers) could afford to lavish more attention to each engine they built.

By 1973, the Alpina 2002tii was available as a complete and fully-developed automobile. Interestingly, that car offered a higher level of performance than the factory built 2002 Turbo. While both cars were actually very close in terms of acceleration and top speed, the naturally-aspirated Alpina was a considerably more comfortable and enjoyable car to drive. With the Alpina car, there was no turbo lag to interfere with the driving experience (a significant problem with the 2002 Turbo), and fuel consumption was much lower—almost 2 liters less per 100 kilometer. Additionally, the Alpina 2002tii was priced at approximately 1500 DM less than the factory car.

Their 2002 product range represented a significant and ongoing success for Alpina, allowing them to prosper during a period of difficulty for the industry. With the oil crisis beginning to take effect, many large and powerful cars were proving difficult to sell—and were being eliminated from manufacturers' lines. At the same time, most larger and inefficient sports cars were depreciating rapidly in the used car market. During the mid-1970s, many of the smaller European tuning firms disappeared forever, unable to reconcile their product line to the requirements of the time.

Alpina, however, not only survived but thrived. Their success was due in large part to the company's willingness to adapt modern technology to traditional tuning techniques. Alpina's ability to extract power from smaller engines (now running on lower octane fuels), provided them with products well suited to the needs of their customers.

With the continued success of Alpina's tuning business, Bovensiepen moved more aggressively towards the concept of providing their customers with complete cars. He recalls, "After 15 years of operating as a top tuning company, we made the strategic decision to concentrate on building our own cars."

In a real sense, the company's change in direction reflected the demands of the market; just building more horsepower was no longer enough. For Bovensiepen, BMW's introduction of the 3.0CSL (fitted from new with many Alpina-developed components) represented the culmination of his years of work. For Alpina, BMW's introduction of the CSL not only provided them with a superb advertisement for their products, but also served to more fully legitimize their efforts. With a selling price of about 43,000 DM, and with impressive performance and build quality, the CSL compared favorably with cars such as the Aston Martin DBS V-8 and the Ferrari 365 GT 2+2 (both of which sold from between 75,000 and 80,000 DM).

Concurrent with the introduction of the CSL, Alpina gained considerably greater access to BMW's dealer network; now Alpina wheels, spoilers and accessories were sold and installed by BMW dealers with the full support of the factory. Alpina-equipped BMWs could be made to resemble (and perform like) the highly successful race and rally cars.

While the decision to proceed with separate, fully-developed Alpina models was made early on, the actual introduction of such a car was not made until 1978. In that year, Bovensiepen chose a handful of motoring journalists to demonstrate his newest creation—the 3-series based Alpina B6 (officially available from November of 1978). What the company had done was to install BMW's larger 6-cylinder engine (here at 2.8-liters) into their smallest car. With 200bhp motivating a relatively small, light car, the results were dramatic—setting the stage for numerous later Alpina projects.

The larger engined 3-series was a success both in terms of its abilities and the attention it brought to Alpina. The B6 was notably unlike the majority of powerful sporting cars of the late-1970s; the Alpina-modified BMW was smooth and relaxed in daily driving, but with an immense reserve of power and torque. In almost every way (except perhaps for its initial cost), the B6 improved upon the platform provided by BMW's excellent 3-series.

The concept of a small BMW with a large engine appealed to BMW of South Africa, who incorporated Alpina's engineering and components to build their own BMW 333i. Following that project, BMW Germany built their own 3.2-liter version of the 3-series with the Alpina logo cast onto the intake manifolds.

Alpina followed their success with the 3-series with what was probably the most potent 4-door sedan of the period. Based on BMW's 5-series sedan, Alpina's B7 Turbo offered 300 horsepower in a very low-key package. The most visible indications that the car was in any way different from a standard 518i were the Alpina side stripes and the wide aluminum alloy wheels. The trunk lid carried the Alpina name and the B7 Turbo designation—a wolf in sheep's clothes.

Alpina's development of turbocharged BMW engines was conducted under the direction of Dr. Fritz Indra. Dr. Indra later became head of engine development at Audi, and is now the director of Advanced Development Projects at GM's Opel subsidiary in Russelsheim, Germany. For Alpina Dr. Indra created turbocharged applications which combined both enormous torque and high specific horsepower—allowing his engines to provide exceptional performance and flexibility.

Alpina's previous work made clear that increased horsepower without concurrent improvements throughout the car was of little value. Given the state of suspension technology circa 1980, Alpina's creations could not avoid a firm (and even stiff) ride quality. The company built their cars to thrive at extremely high rates of speed (even if many owners would never use their full potential), and as such sacrificed some degree of compliance in favor of dynamic ability.

Interestingly, most of the suspension tests for the B7 were conducted under a long-term program supervised by both the TUV and BMW's own R&D department. As part of that program, the turbocharged car was required to run 10,000 kilometers at full race speeds on the north side of the

Nurenburg Ring. Despite the severity of the test, the B7 revealed no faults whatsoever. Performance testing of the car produced a top speed in excess of 260 kilometers per hour, with acceleration from 0-100 kilometer per hour taking less than 6.0 seconds.

In principal, the function of a turbocharger seems simple enough; just bolt on the device and enjoy the benefits. The reality is much more complex. As is generally known, proper turbocharged applications take a great deal of time to develop. The balancing of variables such as compression, turbo boost and engine management systems are critical if the engine is to provide power with longevity. Because turbochargers provide non-linear power increases (proportionally higher power gains at higher rpms), striking a balance between high-rpm power and low-rpm driveability becomes somewhat difficult.

With BMW's development of the M1 sports car, and with that car's 25-valve engine moving into production with the M5, the factory moved to provide their customers with some measure of what had previously been available only from Alpina. Despite increased power available directly from the BMW factory, Alpina continued to offer turbocharged alternatives which often outperformed the factory cars (and which provided a generally different driving experience).

As an indication of the quality of their work, Alpina has operated since 1983 as a Registered Automobile Manufacturer in Germany. After over 25 years of developing BMW's 6-cylinder engine, the company continues to extract even greater power and reliability from that motor.

After the single-turbo 5-series B7 cars (both E-12 and E-28 based), Alpina began a program of fitting twin turbochargers to their top performance models. With the new E-34 5-series (also available from Alpina without turbochargers), the company offered 360bhp in a practical and efficient package. Available from August 1989 to March 1993 (with a total of 507 built), the twin-turbocharged 5-series provided a level of engine responsiveness which would have been impossible with a single larger unit. Turbo lag is largely a function of the time it takes for a turbocharger unit to begin spinning. With two smaller and lighter units, there exists a proportional decrease in that time, and in turbo lag. While extremely advanced for its time, the Alpina single turbocharger motor (as with al-

Two different views of the Alpina lineup, circa 1986. Above: the B9 3.5 (based on the E-28 5-series), the B6 2.8 (based on the E-30 3-series) and the B7 Turbo (based on the 6-series coupe).

most all such installations) could be difficult to drive, especially on wet or slippery roads. The twin turbo engine was far more driver-friendly, providing power and lower RPMs and with a significantly wider power band.

At the 1988 Geneva Auto Show, Alpina exhibited their 360bhp B7 Biturbo 5-series next to the Ferrari Testarossa (then probably the most expensive production sports car in the world). While the B7 appeared to be very much like any other BMW 5-series next to the exotic Ferrari, it is noteworthy that a contemporary road test by *Auto Motor und Sport* found that the Alpina sedan fully matched the performance (both acceleration and top speed) of the Testarossa.

Alpina continued to move forward with the development of their turbocharged motors. With the goal of improving engine flexibility and top-gear responsiveness, the company developed sophisticated and fully electronic engine management systems. In addition to their inclusion as

This photo shows slightly later versions of the same cars.

standard equipment on complete Alpina cars, the company's electronic control systems were available on an aftermarket basis.

In 1985, the German Government began discussions which would ultimately lead to the fitting of catalytic converters on all cars sold in that country. In response, Alpina moved to incorporate those devices on all their cars. While many larger cars of that period were equipped with ceramic-lined catalytic converters, Alpina's were lined with platinum and Rhodium—materials which better suited the cars' high-performance characteristics (Porsche used similar catalysts).

With BMW having significantly broadened their product line by the mid-1980s, Alpina also moved to increase the number of complete cars they offered. Currently, the base Alpina model is the 3-series based B3, incorporating a 204bhp 2.7-liter motor. That car is offered in 2-door, 4-door and convertible configurations. (Alpina also made that same engine available in the short-lived BMW Z1 sportscar.) Alpina's next step up is their 3.5-liter B6 motor (with 254bhp), available in the 3-series (and previously in the first-generation M3).

Alpina offers the same 3.5-liter B6 motor in BMW's current-generation 5-series (with a complete set of Alpina modifications). Also available is the B10 (Bi-Turbo) version of the 5-series. At the top of Alpina's 5-series range is the B12 5.0, incorporating BMW's V-12 engine (tuned by Alpina for 350bhp). The continued success of their most powerful model (approximately 30 percent of the company's current production is accounted for by B12s), proves that there still exists a market for such cars. The company went so far as to develop a 4-turbocharger variation of the V-12 engine. Unfortunately, Alpina's R&D group were unable to find the space to install the engine. While Karl Otto Noelle (the engineer responsible for the project) acknowledged that such an installation was not possible, he noted that the Alpina-tuned naturally aspirated V-12 provides exceptional power.

Alpina notes that in addition to offering some of the world's best cars, the company also provides a range of exceptional wines. While small, that business is nonetheless highly significant for the Alpina. Of the company's operating income of about 90 million DM annually, approximately 10 percent is reinvested in their wine operations. Made from grapes grown in Italian vineyards, Alpina's wines are available in European restaurants and also for export (current export markets include both Asia and the U.S.), and have received numerous favorable reviews.

HIGH-PERFORMANCE BMWs: OTHER EFFORTS

The basic virtue of BMW production cars has encouraged the development of an industry dedicated to improving them still further. While Alpina has historically garnered the most attention, this work would not be complete without mention of those other firms which have had a substantial impact.

Hartage

After several years of successfully tuning competition and road-going BMWs, Herbert Hartage founded Hartage GmbH in 1971 to conduct those activities on a more formal basis.

Officially recognized by the German motor vehicle authorities as an automobile manufacturer since 1983, Hartage occupies a state-of-the-art engineering and manufacturing facility in Beckingen. The factory, set on 16,000 square meters of land, employs a total of 30 people.

It is clear that Hartage maintains a serious commitment to the quality of their engineering and their products. As with other small German tuners, Hartage's English language literature is not so fully developed as their cars. Reprinted here is their stated corporate philosophy with certain clarifications.

> Hartage is synonymous with individually-modified BMW automobiles coupled with the highest standards of quality. The company addresses all aspects of performance, driving behavior and appearance of standard BMW automobiles to meet a broad spectrum of their customers' demands.
>
> The styling of Hartage's aerodynamic parts and aluminum wheels is deliberately restrained. The emphasis here is on engineering and function.
>
> A significant part of the company's product philosophy centers on quality maximization. In 1993, Hartage became the first company in the aftermarket tuning industry to receive the ISO 9000 quality certification.
>
> At Hartage, the foundation of all performance development rests on continuous testing—on the test bench, on the race track and under normal driving conditions. Complete suitability for everyday use and absolute customer satisfaction are the result of intensive development and testing work.
>
> A comprehensive customer service program (including conversions, same-day engine tuning,

transport service, etc.) and the highest standards of craftsmanship are further Hartage hallmarks.

Hartage performance conversions meet the strictest environmental and emission regulations. Through increases in power and maximum torque, Hartage automobiles have larger performance reserves -contributing to active safety under all conditions.

Hartage automobiles are built to satisfy the demands of the sporting driver, while maintaining the refinement and quality built into every BMW.

—Hartage GmbH Press Information,
August 1995

Schnitzer

As with most other European tuners, Schnitzer began as a race shop specializing in preparing BMWs. Josef Schnitzer started racing a modified BMW 1800Ti in hillclimbs and circuit races in 1964, and was runner-up in the German Champi-onship that year. Over time, Josef and his brother Herbert Schnitzer came to offer special race-developed components for customers to use on their street cars (perhaps the best known of those components being their 4-cylinder (2002 era) engine conversions, including their enormously effective 4-valve cylinder head). In 1966, the brothers opened a BMW showroom in Freilassing, the same year in which Josef Schnitzer became German Circuit Race Champion in his 1800Tisa and 2000Ti. The following year, the company began running their motorsport effort on a more formal basis, under the name "Team Schnitzer." During the 1970s and 1980s, Schnitzer GmbH produced a range of high-performance products for road-going BMWs (and also a limited number of fully-modified road cars), but the emphasis was primarily on competition activities. In 1987, the company signed a contract with a large German BMW dealer, Kohl Automobile GmbH, covering the worldwide marketing of Schnitzer's road car tuning range under the name "AC Schnitzer." Since that time, the activities of the

A Hartage M3 rally car in action. With special tuning, these cars produced 296bhp at 8,400rpm, and distinguished themselves in competition.

tuning company (AC Schnitzer) and the race team (Schnitzer GmbH) have been conducted separately.

AC Schnitzer today produces both high-performance BMW components and complete vehicles. The company's products are available through over 50 BMW dealerships, primarily in Germany.

THE U.S. TUNERS

The success of the German BMW tuners (combined with demand from U.S. customers) has encouraged a number of U.S. companies to provide similar systems and programs. While the efforts of these U.S. companies were often built on German-supplied components, several companies offered tuning packages which were comparable to those available in Europe. We have listed those companies whom we believe have contributed the most to the world of BMW performance tuning.

Callaway Turbosystems

Located in Old Lyme, CT, Callaway Turbosystems (now Callaway Cars) has built a strong reputation for their conversion work on a variety of cars. The company, run by Reeves Callaway, began as an aftermarket provider of well-designed aftermarket turbosystems and progressed to OEM relationships with companies such as General Motors (with the twin-turbocharged Callaway Corvette),

Herbert Schnitzer, seen here with one of his most successful race cars—the BMW/Schnitzer 635CSi.

Dieter Quester in the Schnitzer 3.0CSL at Le Mans in 1976.

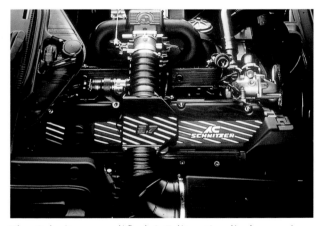

The Schnitzer-modified 3.7-liter 6-cylinder engine, good for 262bhp with catalytic converter.

Right
The Schnitzer-modified 3-liter engine, shown here on the company's test bed.

and to advanced military contracting projects. From the late-1970s to the mid-1980s, Callaway offered U.S. BMW owners some of the best engineered turbo systems available anywhere.

Available for both four and six-cylinder BMWs, the Callaway systems provided dramatic increases in performance. Installed in an otherwise standard U.S.-specification 633csi, the Callaway system enabled the car to accelerate from 0-60 miles per hour in a scant 6.5 seconds (stock was 8.4 seconds).

While these systems were aftermarket in the sense that there existed no formal relationship between BMW and Callaway, the company's cars (especially those which they prepared themselves) were certainly a step above the usual aftermarket turbo system available at that time. In the company's own words;

> *The Callaway Turbocharger System for BMW six cylinder cars places the turbocharger on the right side of the engine block, carefully nesting in the lower part of the engine compartment. While this placement makes manufacturing the conversion more difficult, it has numerous benefits. It concentrates the heat of the turbocharger in an area where it can receive good airflow and can not harm delicate components. It places the turbocharger into a very short exhaust routing necessary to maximize heat and energy utilization. It also removes the turbocharger from any of the normally serviced areas such as valve adjustment and spark plug changing. However, we left the electronic fuel injection's airflow sensor in its stock location. The airflow starts by passing through a specially modified BMW air filter canister, providing ease of maintenance and silent filtration. The airflow is then ducted through aluminum castings to the compressor inlet of a Rotomaster TO4b Turbocharger.*
>
> —Callaway Turbosystems
> company literature, 1982

A visit to Callaway Cars several years ago (after the company had exited the aftermarket turbo business) revealed a remarkable operation. At that time, the company was concentrating on the last of their twin-turbocharged Corvettes (and the radical Corvette-based Speedster). With one Speedster and several individual engines being carefully con-

structed in an environment of meticulous care, the operation was clearly that of a specialty manufacturer. Most immediately noticeable was the fact that the facility was surgically clean, with all work being done by people who seemed to place a high level of importance on their duties. A tour of the facility revealed an inventory of miscellaneous vintage BMW tuning equipment, including a one-of-a-kind turbosystem for a BMW motorcycle. While Callaway has moved on from their aftermarket turbosystem origins, it is clear that the company is still proud of that body of work.

With Callaway having done OEM turbo work for GM, Alfa Romeo (with their factory-authorized U.S.-only twin-turbo GTV6) and Volkswagen, the company's cars tend to blur the line between aftermarket and factory. While not as obviously desirable as a BMW Motorsport or Alpina-prepared car (which would likely have significant modifications made to the entire car, rather then just the engine), a Callaway-prepared BMW would certainly provide a great deal of enjoyment, and might be significantly easier and less-expensive to come by in the U.S.

Dinan Performance Engineering

Although a relatively recent arrival to BMW tuning, Dinan currently enjoys probably the strongest reputation of any U.S.-based company. Based in Mountain View, California, Steve Dinan began where Reeves Callaway left off—with high-quality aftermarket turbosystems for BMWs. Dinan originally offered BMW performance products under the name Bavarian Performance (beginning in 1979). Along with an active motorsport effort, the company now provides complete tuning programs for both early and late model cars. A wide range of engine options are available, including turbocharged, supercharged and increased-displacement motors based on the 5-, 6-, 7- and 8-series BMWs. Dinan has provided M5 and M6 conversions with well over 400bhp, and has produced a twin-turbocharged 8-series with close to 800bhp. The company is perhaps best known for their turbocharged 390bhp M6, a car which was found capable of accelerating from 0-60 miles per hour in only 4.8 seconds. That same car reached a recorded top speed of 172 miles per hour.

Along with greater horsepower, Dinan offers a complete and well-regarded chassis tuning program, with their own line of springs, shocks, sway bars and bushings and alloy wheels. Dinan maintains a large and loyal customer base, with cars sent to their shop from around the world.

Korman Autoworks

Ray Korman began racing BMWs in 1966 (with an 1800ti), and accumulated an enormous number of victories (in a wide range of BMWs) over the next 30 years. In 1977, Korman started Korman Autoworks to sell racing and high-performance street equipment to like-minded BMW enthusiasts. Throughout the 1970s and 1980s, the company was one of the few sources for knowledgeable advice and service, as well as for difficult-to-find equipment from the European tuners. Today, Korman offers performance components from Alpina, Schnitzer and many other suppliers. The company also manufactures street and racing equipment to their own specifications and prepares customers' cars. Korman is located in Greensboro, North Carolina.

The F1600 Project

Korman Autoworks figured prominently in the creation of one of the most impressive BMW specials ever built: the late Joe Bill Dryden's highly modified 1600ti. The car began as a 1968 BMW 1600ti (the factory high-performance version of the standard 1600 two-door sedan). Mr. Dryden developed the car over the next 25 years, employing most of the relevant high-performance techniques and components as they became available. Korman became involved several years ago, and rebuilt the car to incorporate state-of-the-art technology and build standards. In its current form, the car uses an M6 engine with a special Korman engine management chip (good for in excess of 300bhp). The chassis has undergone major modifications, and now includes tubular steel bars reinforcing the front corners of the engine compartment, the front frame rails and the lower front subframe. The F1600's braking system includes Tii front struts with special Alpina ventilated rotors and Korman brake pads. At the rear, Korman supplied their 250mm brake drum conversion. The body incorporates a Korman Kevlar front hood with Zender fender flares front and rear. The car's suspension consists of 2.5-inch diameter racing springs with Korman sway bars and bushings. The battery was relocated to the trunk for better weight distribution.

With a power-to-weight ratio of approximately 9:1, performance is fully the equal of almost anything which has been made road-legal. While detailing all of the special equipment and features which went into creating the F1600 is beyond the scope of this work, the car serves as an excellent example of the best of those cars built by capable enthusiasts with the help of BMW tuners.

HIGH PERFORMANCE BMWs: THE CARS

While the BMW models discussed in this book were made in relatively small numbers, their impact on the company and their worldwide reputation should not be underestimated. Even in the U.S., where almost none of the most interesting models were ever made available, this impact was widely felt. Although invisible in U.S BMW showrooms throughout the 1970s and most of the 1980s, those very few special model BMWs which were privately imported became objects of immense interest, eagerly examined by the motoring press and (if their virtue was not diminished by the process of complying with U.S. safety and emission standards) greatly appreciated by enthusiastic owners.

While this work is intended as an analysis of BMW's *high-performance* road cars, the relationship between those cars and the company's competition efforts is ever present. As such, we have tried to include information regarding those efforts where appropriate.

These then are the cars which not only helped to build BMW's current reputation, but which provided their owners with an enjoyment and pride of ownership which only comes with something exceptional.

CHAPTER 3

Early High-Performance Efforts:
The Four-Cylinder Cars

THE FIRST STEP: THE 1800TiSA

BMW's first legitimate effort at post-war reconstruction took the form of a seemingly modest, 4-door, 4-cylinder sedan (to be called the new class). This car, originally called the 1500 and fitted with a 1.5 liter 4-cylinder, effectively formed the basis of all the company's subsequent efforts from that point to today. Setting the stage for almost every other BMW sedan, the original design was both mature and capable of supporting significant additional development. The new class range would extend through several interesting variations, cumulating with the fully-developed 1800Ti and 2000Ti. An analysis of these vehicles today (especially against their competition of the time) reveals how enormously advanced they were at the time of their introduction.

While the 1800Ti sedan represented BMW's first post-war attempt at a high-performance version of an existing production car, the 1800TiSA was a considerably more aggressive effort. For that car, the factory supplied an array of exotic (for the time) components incorporated into the basic New Class platform. The 1800TiSA featured a stiffer suspension (which lowered the car), a close-ratio 5-speed gearbox, large (45mm) DCOE Webber carburetors and a higher-life camshaft. The

BMW's 2002 Turbo. The factory's most potent road-going version of the popular 2002.

The BMW 1800Ti, originally introduced at the 1963 Frankfurt Automobile Show. With 110bhp, and with a top speed of 170 kilometers per hour, the car was described as a touring sports sedan—a category BMW essentially invented. The rare 1800TiSA was based on this model.

An 1800 TiSA at speed in the 1965 Monte Carlo Rally.

TiSA also incorporated lightened bodywork with specially made thinner-gauge panels.

Although the 1800 TiSA was never intended for road use (sales were typically restricted to active racing teams), the car was built to be entirely road-legal, and there was no reason why it could not be so used. Especially after becoming obsolete for racing purposes (a process which never takes more than a few years), many cars found their ways onto the street. In that capacity, and in the mid-1960s, the TiSA was a better sport sedan than almost anything else available. BMW today makes a fine range of cars (including some which are truly exceptional [i.e., the M3]), but it is doubtful that the margin of superiority which the TiSA enjoyed over other small sedans in the mid- to late-1960s will ever be duplicated. The company produced only the 200 vehicles required for homogenization of the TiSA.

The 1967 2000CS—BMW's first sports coupe based on a totally post-war design.

The format established by BMW (with the 1800TiSA and 2000Ti) of building lightweight, but properly-engineered and constructed vehicles has never really been abandoned. Inspection of an original example of one of these cars today reveals a very high level of fit and finish, combined with almost modern levels of performance and handling. That these vehicles, which are now almost 30 years old, should compare so well with currently available cars says a great deal about how they compared with their contemporaries.

Today, the 1800Ti, 2000Ti, 2000TiLux and 2000Tii cars are all desirable examples of BMW's first post-war sports sedans. While somewhat difficult to find (especially in good condition), any of these would represent an interesting 4-door alternative to a (mechanically similar) 2002. An original 1800 TiSA is far less likely to see regular use on the street; those cars will generally be used in vintage racing (for which they are eligible), or reside in collections.

THE ALPINA 2000CS

The 2000CS, BMW's first modern postwar coupe, was introduced in 1966 as an extension to the successful New Class range. Built (by Karmann) upon that line's well-proven chassis, the coupe was essentially a stylish 2-door version of the 2000. With the car's otherwise elegant lines compromised by an unusual and somewhat severe front-end treatment, together with a price comparable to contemporary Porsches, the new car appealed to a limited audience. Dynamically, the 4-cylinder coupe stood on very firm ground by the standards of the mid-1960s. Driving impressions of the car today reveal a light, agile car with a level of sensitivity remarkable given its age. With the standard 2-liter, 120 horsepower engine, performance is somewhat inferior to a stock 2002, but not so much so that the car feels significantly underpowered. Also notable is the overall level of comfort provided; with a relatively lightweight,

31

Although the car was heavier than the 2000 Sedan with which it shared its engine, 2000CS performance was still quite good. Alpina's first coupe was based on this car.

long wheelbase (relative to the 02 cars) and not very aggressive suspension rates, the 2000CS makes for very relaxed cruising.

With the introduction of the 2002 (which used the same engine in a lighter body), and with growing criticism of the coupe's lackluster performance in comparison with other cars in the same price range, BMW clearly felt the need to reposition their most expensive car.

The solution came as it had before and has ever since—through a visit to the corporate parts bin. By 1969, the 4-cylinder coupe had been stretched and reworked into the 2800CS. This new car used the company's inline, 2.8-liter 6-cylinder engine, eliminating any performance concerns while providing the basis for significant future development (see below). While, in retrospect, the transformation may seem to have been made more on the basis of market necessity than engineering desirability, BMW benefited (as they always have) from the soundness of their basic products combined with obsessive attention to detail.

Although the 2000CS is today regarded as an interim model and is given far less attention then the later 6-cylinder coupes, those cars are both beautifully-built and quite enjoyable to use on a regular basis. While often described as underpowered, the 4-cylinder coupe has an excellent balance and a lightness which was largely lost in the later 6-cylinder cars.

While BMW themselves produced no documented higher-performance versions of the

2000CS, Alpina was ready with what is believed to be the company's first full conversion package for an existing vehicle. Contemporary advertisements offer the "BMW 2000CS Alpina" at a price of DM 23,900. For that price, the buyer received Alpina's best efforts; the cars were equipped with the company's competition proven engines (spezialmotor) with two Weber 45 DCOE carburetors (very large), 5-speed gearboxes (almost unheard of for street cars in the mid-1960s), front and rear swaybars, special Koni shock absorbers and special Alpina-Borrani wire wheels with lightweight aluminum rims.

It is not known if any of these Alpina 2000CSs exist in their original state, and we can only speculate on what sort of driving experience one might provide. Based on some familiarity with most of the components utilized in the car, it seems certain that the Alpina version of the 4-cylinder BMW coupe would be significantly faster, better-handling and more entertaining than the stock car. Doubtless, the Alpina coupe would be both notably less comfortable and more temperamental in everyday use (45 DCOEs are probably a bit aggressive for street use).

THE HIGH-PERFORMANCE 02 CARS (TYPE 114)

With the initial success of the new class range, BMW could begin to indulge in competition for the first time since before the war.

Expanding upon the already successful "New Class" range (then consisting of the 1600, 1800 and 2000 sedan models), the company created a smaller and lighter platform using the 1.6-liter engine from the (larger) 1600. This car (also, and confusingly, called the 1600) weighed in at 2100lbs. The car was and remains a masterpiece of miniaturization; in its design, build quality and performance, it was essentially the equal of BMW's larger and more expensive cars. Through the development of the 1600, BMW laid the foundation for 30 years of product evolution.

ALPINA AND THE ORIGIN OF THE 2002; THE 1600 2-LITER

The subtlety of the relationship between Alpina and the BMW factory is perhaps best illustrated by that company's involvement with the 02 platform. Almost as soon as the 1600 became available, Alpina introduced the (dimensionally identical) 2-liter engine to the 1600. The result was remarkable; here was a car with performance which could be legitimately compared with the 2-liter Porsche 911,

but with all the practicality and accommodation of BMW's small sedan.

With their 2 liter version of the 1600, Alpina not only set the stage for 30 subsequent years of tuning efforts, but also provided the Factory with the model for what many consider their most successful product to date; the hugely popular 2002. That car (essentially BMW's own version of the Alpina 02) was formed by the fitting of the 2 liter engine into the 1600, with modifications to handle the additional power. The 2002 was an immediate and enormous success; with virtually every motoring periodical publishing glowing reviews.

Despite the marketing brilliance of Max Hoffman in suggesting the mass projection of the resulting car (the 2002) for the U.S. market, the initial conception and creation of that car clearly belongs to Alpina. Hoffman's (not inconsiderable) contribu-

tion was actually in the articulation of Alpina's idea for broader commercialization.

Although the Alpina 2-liter 1600 and BMW's subsequent 2002 are conceptually and dynamically almost the same car, the Alpina version must be seen as vastly more desirable. Placing each within the context of history, the Alpina conversion represented an enormous leap forward in performance (relative to both the production 1600 and contemporary rivals). While the factory's own 2-liter 02 car was certainly a strong performer, it nonetheless followed in the path established by Alpina's efforts.

In their December 1967 issue, *Car and Driver* magazine tested an Alpina 2-liter 1600 brought into the U.S. by a serviceman back from Germany. That car carried a price (including U.S. delivery) of $5,579.45, or more then double the price of the outwardly-similar 1600 sedan on which the car was based. The magazine subjected this Alpina-converted car to a full road test, realizing 0-60 miles per hour acceleration of 8.3 seconds (compared with 11.4 for the standard 1600), and a top

The basic 2002, shown here with the larger, U.S.-specification bumpers. The 2002 was among the most popular of all post-war BMWs, and formed the basis for much of the company's success during the late 1960s through the 1970s.

BMW's optional alloy wheel for the 2002. These are rare today.

speed of approximately 125 miles per hour (compared with 102 miles per hour for the 1600). Although there was very little externally to differentiate the Alpina-converted car from the standard 1600, the modified car was recognized as something very special by its testers. Even with a price boosted by Alpina's work to close to that of a Porsche 911, the magazine were clearly impressed.

Alpina factory records do not indicate how many 2-liter 1600 conversions the company performed. In any case, the number must be very small. If the car tested by *Car and Driver* remains intact, it must be one of perhaps only several (if not the only) original Alpina 2-liter 1600 remaining in the U.S. Certainly, there can not be more then perhaps a dozen or so remaining worldwide.

The 2002tii

Once the 2-liter engine had been installed within the 02 chassis on a production basis, the factory set about developing and improving the result. By 1971, automotive fuel injection was a relatively well-understood technology; both Mercedes-Benz and Porsche had been fitting it to their cars for several years. For the 2002, BMW surprised many by adopting the Kuglefischer mechanical injection system (fundamentally similar to that fitted to contemporary Porsche 911s), rather than a more fuel-efficient electronic system. Undoubtedly, the decision added

considerably to the appeal of the resulting car—the 2002 tii. Tuned for maximum performance and response, the car left an indelible impression on many who were not previously familiar with BMW's cars. While the 2002tii was not truly a low-volume special (38,703 units were built between 1971 and 1975), the car had a remarkable impact on the overall market. Rather than limit the opportunity for the tuning companies, the 2002tii served to increase interest in high-performance BMWs and in making them still faster.

If the 1600 was revolutionary, than the 2002tii was cathartic. In Europe, even drivers accustomed to small high-performance sedans were enormously impressed by the fuel-injected 2002. In America, the car came as a sensation; perhaps never before did one car enjoy such a significant competitive advantage on the basis of performance, practicality and price.

While the BMW factory is generally given sole credit for the concept and creation of the Kugelfischer-injected 2002, Alpina were offering a Kugelfischer fuel injection kit for the carbureted 2002 at least as early as the fourth quarter of 1970 (at a price of approximately (U.K. Pounds) 600 for the U.K. market). At a time when a standard 2002 sold for (U.K. Pounds) 1,874, the Alpina Kugelfischer conversion represented an additional cost of 32 percent. At that price, it seems unlikely that many such systems were sold (fewer still were probably installed by Alpina). Although it is uncertain if any Alpina-converted cars survive, an original (and documented) pre-2002tii Alpina-built Kugelfischer-injected car would represent a remarkable piece of history.

Given the close relationship between Alpina and the factory, it seems certain that BMW were at least aware of the Alpina fuel-injected cars. As such, and as with the 2002 itself, we must credit Alpina with a significant role in the development of the highly-regarded 2002tii.

Among the most desirable factory options for the 2002 included a (very rare) close-ratio 5-speed Getrag transmission (with a racing-style layout which placed first gear down and towards the driver). This gearbox (which was offered only for the 2002tii) provided drivers with a significantly greater degree of flexibility than with the standard 4-speed. While not necessarily much faster, the 5-speed certainly made the tii more enjoyable. With specially-tuned versions requiring drivers to maintain higher engine speeds, the 5-speed became less of a luxury and more of a necessity.

Probably the second most coveted period 2002 option was and remains a set of original factory alloy wheels. These rims featured a design very similar to those offered on the 2800CS Coupe, and are very difficult to find today. Except for the special Mahle rims offered (optionally) on the 2002 Turbo, these were the only alloy wheels ever offered by the factory for the 2002.

THE ALPINA 2002s

With BMW continually increasing the performance of their production 02 cars during the early 1970s, Alpina had to strive to stay ahead in terms of development. That development took the form of an increasingly wide range of Alpina performance equipment, and the production of complete, fully outfitted Alpina vehicles.

With the company's specialized versions of the 2002, Alpina began to distinguish themselves as an autonomous and separate manufacturer of automobiles, as opposed to an ordinary tuning company. To many, this distinction may be somewhat confusing; Alpina has only ever produced cars based upon production BMWs, and the company's finished products are easily and immediately recognizable as BMWs. Nonetheless, the difference becomes clear when examining a fully converted Alpina; those cars differ from their regular production counterparts in both their construction and their purpose.

In terms of establishing provenance, Alpina's 2002s can present difficulties. As with all of that company's early efforts, records appear to have been kept on the basis of engines, rather than on complete cars. Those factory records do indicate where the Alpina engines were to be installed—differentiating between identical engines intended for different models. We would advise prospective owners to carefully check all documentation accompanying any early car with Alpina credentials. While it may be impossible to establish authenticity on the basis of serial numbers, cars prepared by Alpina themselves were typically provided with detailed paperwork attesting to all work done.

ALPINA AND THE 2002:
ORDERING A LA CARTE

While customers may, even today, order their cars from Alpina in a fairly wide range of configura-

tions, an original 2002 customer was afforded a far greater range of options. In the early-1970s, Alpina's business revolved around the manufacture and fitting of specially-made high-performance parts, rather than the creation of fully-outfitted automobiles. With the 2002, it was still necessary for the customer to specify which components were desired. Given the range of options available from Alpina, that customer would have been able to assemble a remarkable car—as many did.

ENGINES

Excluding their very earliest products (the A1, for which no reliable figures are available), Alpina produced complete engines for the 2002 between July 1969 and May 1986. The engines ran in several distinct series, and were referred to (in ascending order of power and tune) as the A1, A2, A3 and A4 motors.

In a 1972 English-language Alpina brochure, the company offered the following:

Performance-increased 4-cylinder Engines

The price of an ALPINA special engine is to be understood for the conversion of a new BMW engine. If the engine has already been used the price increases by DM 200, if it has already been operating for less than 10,000 km (6200 miles), by DM 500, if it has been in operation for more than 10,000 km. In case the cylinder head, crankcase or crankshaft have been damaged to such an extent that they are no longer usable, these parts will be charged separately. The same applies to parts which are missing on arrival of the engine.

BMW-ALPINA special engine, 2 ltr., 150 DIN H.P., with TI-pistons, 2 Weber double carburetors, special cylinder head with sports camshaft, retouched crank gear, engine completely reassembled, top speed 200 km/h (125 mph) . . . . .2500 DM

Extra charge for lightened and polished connecting rods . . . . .280 DM

Special exhaust system for ALPINA special engine 150 DIN H.P. . . . . .230 DM

BMW-ALPINA special engine, 2 ltr., 165 DIN H.P., with forged pistons, 2 Weber double carburetors 45 DCOE, special cylinder head with larger inlet- and exhaust valves and sport

The interior of an Alpina-modified 2002. Seen here are the Alpina leather-wrapped steering wheel, special additional gauges and deep bucket seats. All of these components are today very difficult to find.

camshaft, retouched crank gear, rallye exhaust system and air cleaner, top speed exceeding 205 km/h (128 mph) . . . . *3700 DM*

CHASSIS COMPONENTS

While Alpina still produces a limited number of components for the 2002, most of the more desirable Alpina accessories for that model have not been made for many years, and are today hoarded by fortunate enthusiasts. Among these rare components are the special *3-piece* alloy race wheels which sometimes (but apparently not very often) accompanied the company's full conversions of the 2002. These wheels, of which perhaps only a few remain in existence, came in two styles. The early design was a very attractive 10-spoke design with the Alpina name set twice into the background pattern. The later wheel introduced the turbine-blade rim style which was adopted by

The engine of an original Alpina 2002. Although not in concours condition, most of the important components are visible.

BMW themselves (and produced in the millions), and which has become perhaps Alpina's most immediately recognizable trademark. Complete sets of these wheels in good condition today command *very* high prices.

SCHNITZER AND THE 2002

Throughout the 1970s, Schnitzer was a name more closely associated with racing than with street cars. While Alpina may also have been better known for their race cars during that period, Schnitzer-derived street cars appear to have been few and far between. That said, the company did produce some remarkable components (again, primarily for competition) some of which were suitable for road-going applications.

Representing probably the most exotic (and expensive) single component available from any source for the 2002 was a Schnitzer 4-valve cylinder head (or even a complete Schnitzer engine). While the great majority of those engines were fitted to competition cars, several were apparently mated to road cars.

Today, 2002 owners who desire the ultimate in performance gravitate towards the installation of a later (4-cylinder) M3 engine (a design, ironically, inspired by the original Schnitzer engines). As such, the demand for early 4-valve Schnitzer power plant components has diminished significantly (the market value of Schnitzer heads apparently fell during the late 1980s with the availability of

used M3 engines). Nonetheless, an original Schnitzer-outfitted 2002 (especially with documentation) would certainly represent an enormously desirable vehicle. A road-going 4-valve Schnitzer car would probably be the definitive performance-modified 2002.

THE FACTORY RAISES THE STAKES:
THE 2002 TURBO

There can be no doubt that BMW had Group 5 racing very much in mind during the development of their road-going 2002 Turbo. The 1972 road-going Turbo was a direct descendent of the turbocharged 275-horsepower 2002 that won the 1969 European Touring Car Championship.

The production 2002 Turbo benefited from a concerted program of chassis upgrades. Larger wheels and tires (185/70VR13s on 5 1/2 in. rims) required large fender flares—the car's most immediately noticeable feature. Also provided were a five-speed gearbox (optional), front and rear sway-bars, more robust shock absorbers and a limited-slip differential. All of this, however, was supplied only in support of the car's most important component—its 170bhp turbocharged engine. BMW's promotional literature states plainly; "The principal item of the BMW 2002 Turbo is the engine."

With a maximum speed of 131 miles per hour, and with the ability to accelerate from 0-100 kilometers per hour in 6.9 seconds, the 2002 Turbo was clearly fast. Extracting that performance, how-

Walter Rohrl driving the Schnitzer 2002 Turbo in the heat of competition.

The 2002 Turbo—outwardly similar to the standard 2002, but heavily modified underneath. With a turbocharged, 170bhp engine, the car was unquestionably fast. Turbo lag, however, made harnessing that power sometimes difficult.

ever, was less straightforward than with many other cars. Given the relatively primitive stage of automotive turbo development by the mid-1970s, the turbocharged 2002 could not help but suffer from fairly massive turbo lag. In order to prevent detonation, the factory had lowered the car's compression ratio from 9.0:1 (on the U.S. tii) to only 6.9:1. That change, in conjunction with a turbo which did not provide meaningful boost until about 4500rpm, meant that owners had to work very hard indeed to extract the car's performance.

While the 2002 Turbo represents the ultimate factory production-based development of the 02 platform, it is not necessarily the best choice for an enthusiast today. Unmodified, the car would likely be outrun by a well-tuned naturally aspirated car,

The 2002 Turbo at speed at BMW's test track in Germany. Following close behind is a rare 3.0 CSL Batmobile.

and would be much more difficult to drive. In view of the highly sophisticated turbo systems available today, the idea of modifying the 2002 Turbo's induction systems to permit more usable performance is well-founded. There is currently at least one company (Jaymac in England) performing those modifications, with the results having been well-received.

SPECIFIC CARS
2002 Alpina

During the production of this book, I was fortunate to have access to one of only a small handful of U.S.-based 2002s which had been originally and fully modified by Alpina in Germany. While the car (chassis #3668384, Alpina engine #1234) was in far from immaculate condition—a restoration is currently underway—it was an original and basically sound vehicle. Used as an example, #384 provides an almost perfect representation of what Alpina created for their well-healed (and mostly European) customers in the early-to mid-1970s.

Over the course of a high-speed ride along narrow winding roads (at speeds of up to 75 miles per hour on roads marked for 25 miles per hour), the car was immediately and obviously different from any unmodified 2002.

Against the sea of everyday 2002s, #384 is immediately identified as something different. Like U.S.-specification 1974 cars, #384 has square taillights (the change from round to square taillights, combined with much larger U.S.-market bumpers and certain mechanical changes represented a line of demarcation for serious 2002 enthusiasts). Unlike almost any other 2002 in the U.S., #384 combines that feature with (European) small chrome bumpers and large factory-issue Alpina fender flares.

It should be noted that Alpina's exceptional work did not come cheaply; the bill of sale for #384 (dated January 18, 1974) indicates a price (from Alpina) of DM 34,812.40.

The interior compartment of the 2002 Turbo differed only subtly from the regular production version. A smaller leather-wrapped steering wheel as well as more deeply contoured seats are visible.

The turbocharged version of the 2002's engine is remarkably similar to the naturally aspirated version, and is relatively uncluttered by modern standards.

CHAPTER 4

The Move Upmarket:
High-Performance Early 6-Cylinder Sedans and Coupes

THE EARLY 6-CYLINDER SEDANS (E-3)

BMW's encore to their successful range of 4-cylinder cars was a significantly larger car, designed to place the company in direct competition with Mercedes Benz. Previously, the two companies had very little overlap in terms of their product ranges: Mercedes sold large and mid-sized luxury cars (and taxies); while BMW were known for their smaller cars. With the introduction of the company's new E-3 cars, that situation changed permanently. The E-3 line (which included the 2500, 2800, Bavaria, 3.0 (S, Si, L and Li), and 3.3Li models) marked the beginning of BMW's participation at the top level of European luxury automobile manufacturing.

The new large sedans were well-received, and contributed significantly to BMW's growing success. Unlike the 2002, however, the E-3 platform did not lend itself so obviously to high-performance tuning efforts (at least from a marketing perspective). Due not only to its smaller size and lighter weight, but also to its position in the market, the 2002 attracted the significant majority of those customers interested in tuning. Customers purchasing the large 4-door cars were typically more interested in comfort and refinement than in ultimate performance. That said, there were several options available to an early BMW enthusiast who was set on a large sedan.

There were 167 Batmobiles built in total, all of which were finished in either Polaris silver or Chamonix white.

THE 3.0Si

In the late-1960s to mid-1970s, the 3.0Si would have been included in any discussion of leading luxury/performance sedans. During that time, however, Mercedes-Benz (the company's principal competitor) had available a special version of their largest S-Class car. This car, called the 300 SEL 6.3, was created through the installation of the Mercedes' 6.3-liter V-8 engine from their huge 600 limousine in their 4-door 300 SEL sedan. Although it is unlikely that many buyers of the hugely expensive, limited edition Mercedes made direct or careful comparisons with BMW 3.0Si, the importance of the comparison in the minds of the motoring public should not be underestimated. Since well before World War II, Mercedes and BMW have directly competed for customers, often with products very similar in specification. Since that time, the two firms have been keenly aware of each other's activities and have often viewed the other as their primary competitor. Since the 1960s, however, BMW products have usually been easily distinguished from their Mercedes counterparts. In a comparison, the BMW would generally be lighter, more agile and generally somewhat less expensive than the Mercedes, while perhaps lacking some small measure of the Mercedes' remarkable indestructibility. If these observations are generalizations, they would not likely encounter much argument.

A comparison today of the (standard) 3.0Si with the 300 SEL 6.3 reveals the Mercedes to be clearly the faster car (although not by much). It also reveals the BMW to be the much more enjoyable car. Based upon reasonably extensive experience with various examples of both cars, there is little doubt that the 3.0Si is by far the more sporting and involving of the two.

Today, the E-3 cars are generally regarded as somewhat stodgy. They were never raced to the extent as other models from the same period, and were usually sold to buyers with less then sporting intentions. Although most 3.0Sis were destined to be driven slowly (though probably appreciatively), some buyers did recognize the opportunities offered by BMW's largest car.

THE EARLY ALPINA SEDANS 2500 - 3.0Si

If the standard factory 6-cylinder sedans of 1969-1976 were notably superior to their competition, then the Alpina efforts on that same platform were truly remarkable. For all of that car's ability, actually finding an Alpina 3.0Si in 1975/1976 would have required a great deal of work. Whereas the purchase of a Mercedes 300SEL 6.3 demanded only the signing of a very large check, it is unlikely that many BMW dealerships outside of Germany (let alone many potential buyers) were even aware of the Alpina sedan.

At (U.K. Pounds) 2,700, Alpina's conversion to the 3.0Si represented a significant additional expense on top of that car's list price of (U.K. Pounds) 4,299. At (U.K. Pounds) 7,000, the finished Alpina 3.0Si was more expensive then the factory 3.0CSi (at (U.K. Pounds) 6,200, and almost as much as the limited-production 3.0CSL at (U.K. Pounds) 7,400. For their considerable expenditure, buyers received a comprehensively engineered package based upon Alpina's extensive experience at the highest levels of production-based racing.

As Alpina's E-3-based cars preceded the company's system of ascribing separate (Alpina) serial numbers to their completed cars, determining which cars were converted becomes more difficult. While Alpina records from that period track engines, rather then chassis, they distinguish between the model of car for which those engines were intended. Based upon those records, it appears that Alpina built 172 engines between February 1971 and July 1979 for E-3-based cars. All of those engines (which were designated as Alpina's B3) are listed as being of the same capacity (3-liters) and developing the same power (230bhp).

In Alpina's version of the 3.0Si, BMW had a car which was faster, much better handling and even more exclusive than Mercedes' 300 SEL 6.3. From a marketing viewpoint, it is unfortunate that so few were built (or that those that were built were not given broader coverage in the automotive press; the cars would have certainly acquitted themselves brilliantly in any comparison test). Because no records of the Alpina-prepared E-3s remain cataloged by that company, documentation of Alpina's work on a particular car becomes more important. For the collector able to locate one of these rare sedans, it represents not only a desirable example of an early tuner car, but also an entirely worthwhile vehicle for regular use.

THE EARLY 6-CYLINDER COUPES: OVERVIEW

While the E-9 coupe was probably the most aesthetically perfect BMW to date, the car suffered, in some ways, by comparison with its less glamorous four-door sibling. Because the 6-cylinder coupe was directly descended from the earlier 2000CS (itself derived from the 1500/2000 series of four-door sedans), the car represented a dynamically less complete package relative to cars designed from a clean sheet—such as the 3.0Si.

The first series coupes (the 2.8-liter 2800CSs) were not equipped with 4-wheel disk brakes; rear drums were fitted until the introduction of the 3.0-liter 3.0CS in 1972. Perhaps more importantly, the coupes' elegant profile was achieved by the pillarless design of its greenhouse. While the lack of a B-pillar contributed greatly to the coupes' beauty, it extracted a price in terms of torsional rigidity.

Despite any limitations the coupes' hybrid origins may have represented, the development lavished upon them put them far ahead of any of the company's other offerings. For many years (and even after the introduction of the 6-series coupe), the E-9 coupe remained BMW's primary weapon for production-class racing.

THE E-9 ALPINA COUPES

With the introduction of the 2800CS in 1969, BMW took a significant step up market. The company's first 6-cylinder coupe represented the company's move into a market historically ruled by Porsche, Mercedes, Jaguar and a handful of others. Dynamically, the early coupes differed little from their less glamorous sedan counterparts. Even so, contemporary reviews put those cars on equal footing with their then-rivals.

Even more than the most ardent BMW enthusiasts, Alpina must have greeted the 6-cylinder coupe with tremendous excitement. While the company's previous offerings had successfully combined excellent performance with BMW's traditional build quality and thorough engineering, here finally was a car which reflected its inner quality in its outward appearance. In the opinion of many (the author included), this was and remains BMWs greatest aesthetic success.

While numerous BMWs for the 1970s are today represented either as Alpinas or as Alpina-converted cars, it is noteworthy that the level of Alpina equipment on many of these cars amounts only to superficial items such as wheels and trim. True Alpina cars from that period will have been modified by Alpina (in Germany) to a significant extent.

The 3.0CSi coupe, here undergoing wet-weather testing at the BMW facility. The E-9 coupes (as this series was known) still stand as probably the best looking of all post-war BMWs. The 3-liter coupes formed the basis for subsequent efforts by BMW Motorsport, Alpina and Schnitzer.

Hopefully, the documentation which the company provided to purchasers of their cars will have been retained. As discussed above, cars having received Alpina modifications (even by the company themselves) and no substantive mechanical modifications are not regarded as true Alpinas. By far the most historically significant and desirable 6-cylinder Alpina-modified cars from the 1970s are those with the most comprehensive modifications (those conforming to the specifications of fully-converted Alpina cars). Fully-modified 3.0-Liter coupes and sedans are most importantly distinguished by the addition of Alpina's Kuglefisher mechanical fuel-injection conversion to the 6-cylinder engine (a system used extensively by BMW themselves for racing applications, but never on a

The 3.0CSL, as prepared by Alpina for Group 2 racing. These cars distinguished themselves in production class racing, and added significantly to both BMW's and Alpina's reputations. While the external modifications are obvious enough, Alpina also replaced almost every major mechanical component. The 12-valve, 3.3-liter engine produced between 325bhp and 340bhp. Pictured is driver Bruno Giacomelli.

factory 6-cylinder road car). As with the 2002tii, the mechanical fuel-injection setup endowed the larger 6-cylinder car not only with greater horsepower, but also with a level of responsiveness and immediacy not possible with either the factory carburetion or electronic fuel-injection induction systems fitted to that engine.

One original option fitted to at least a few Alpina-modified coupes was a set of attractive original-design alloy wheels. These rims (which I have seen only in photographs), preceded the company's famous turbine-blade design later adopted by BMW themselves.

THE 3.0CSLs

Unlike their previous 1800TiSA and 2002 Turbo, BMW's third series-built factory special was inspired not only by the requirement for a competition car, but also by a desire to provide customers with a vehicle even more exciting than the standard 3.0CSi. By 1971, BMW's coupe was no longer brand new, and several manufacturers offered cars with superior performance at lower prices.

While the 3.0CSL was clearly meant for competition, the prototype seems to have been a car ordered by Bob Lutz (BMW's Director of Sales at the time) for his personal use. That car (which was tested by several magazines) predated the production CSL, but was very similar to the early series-built cars.

The 3.0CSL might have been BMW's road-going flagship during most of the 1970s, but its reason for being was still tied to its usefulness in competition. As such, and because the car was never intended to be a high-volume product, changes to the model corresponded almost entirely to the requirements of motorsport homologation. 3.0CSLs can essentially be divided into three groups as follows;

Series 1 (serial numbers within regular coupe production): The first CSLs were very much modified 3.0CSs, with no changes whatsoever to the drivetrain. The cars were significantly lightened (by approximately 400 pounds), with the view towards competition activities. Even with the standard 2985cc carbureted engine, these first CSLs were notably quicker than the standard cars and were fully competitive with contemporary rivals. A total of 169 of these were produced.

Series 2 (serial numbers 2275001-2275429): These represent the bulk of non-U.K. market CSL production, with 429 cars built in total. As was the pattern with CSLs, the requirements of competition dictated the primary changes to the car. Series 2 CSLs benefited from fuel injection combined with a small increase in displacement (to 3003cc) to produce 200 horsepower.

Series 2 RHD (serial numbers 2285001-2285500): An interesting derivation of the Series 2 CSLs were the 500 right-hand-drive cars produced for sale in the United Kingdom. A marketing decision by BMW GB determined that CSLs for that market should be more grand tourer (or more practical) and less sports car. As such, those cars were re-equipped with much of the equipment which had originally been removed to make them lighter. UK-market CSLs came with CSi-specification steel bumpers, glass, rather then Plexiglas side-windows and a more luxurious (closer to standard CSi-level) interior. Later cars substituted standard steel panels for the lightweight aluminum hood, trunk lid and doors.

Series 3 (serial numbers 2275430-2275539): Commonly referred to as the Batmobile, the Series 3 CSL took the basic concept of a lighter and stronger BMW coupe one step further. By 1974, BMW Motorsport were eager to homologate their (then) competition-only 3.5-liter engine for production-based racing. That homologation re-

BMW's 3.0CSL Batmobile. These cars differed from the standard 3.0CSLs in that they were fitted with the larger 3.2-liter engines, and were offered with the spoiler package seen here.

quired the production of a run of larger-engined road cars. The result was the fitting of their 3.2-liter (3153 cc) engine to the 3.0CSL which increased horsepower by 6bhp (to 206bhp), and also provided a small increase in torque. In addition to the larger engine, Series 3 cars were in some cases (though not always) supplied with a package of aerodynamic appendages so dramatic that the name "Batmobile" was soon applied. That package consisted of a very large rear wing, a more traditional rear spoiler and front fender spats. Although almost certainly overkill for the street, those components (which were now homologated for production racing) proved enormously valuable in competition. There were 167 Batmobiles built in total (including the series 3.5 cars, see below), all of which were finished in wither Polaris silver or Chamonix white.

Series 3.5 (serial numbers 4355001-4355057): Also Batmobiles, these cars are essentially identical to the Series 3 cars, but incorporated several minor (and mostly cosmetic) changes. There were 57 cars built.

In many ways, the 3.0CSL is the definitive post-war BMW. For anyone with an appreciation of BMW's history, an original 3.0CSL would repre-

The 3.2-liter Batmobile—the fastest and most desirable of all the factory E-9 coupes.

sent a cherished possession. Unfortunately, the cars' lack of any effective rustproofing has lead to a relatively low survival rate. For those able either to locate a pristine car or to fund the restoration of a CSL in need of attention, their efforts should be well-rewarded.

3.0CSL 3.2 DRIVING IMPRESSIONS

For inclusion within this book, we were especially fortunate to have access not just to a 3.0CSL (rare as those are in the U.S.), but to one of the only 167 3.2 examples of the Batmobile version (believed to be one of four residing in the U.S.). The following impressions relate specifically to that car, but may be seen as generally representative of the line.

With a larger 6-cylinder engine than the standard 3.0CSL, and with the full complement of spoilers seen here, this was the ultimate development of the model.

One of the first impressions any driver will have of a 3.0CSL will be the extreme lightness of the door upon entering the cabin. That lightness is a function of its aluminum construction, and is in marked contrast to the much heavier steel items found on the more common 3.0CS/CSis (which generally require a strong pull to open and close). The weight of the driver's door sets the stage for much of the CSL driving experience; the car is similar to the 3.0CSi, but is lighter, faster and more precise than that car. The CSL can essentially be seen as a 3.0CSi with a finer edge.

The CSL's advantages do not come without a price (even beyond the considerable price premium required both when it was new and today). Seen another way, the CSL is a louder, less refined and less comfortable 3.0CSi. With essentially no soundproofing and a significantly stiffer suspension, more of what is happening below and around the car is transmitted directly to the driver. While it is somewhat surprising to find that a car as well-engineered and highly developed as the CSL feels a bit crude, that is indeed much of the car's charm. It is especially interesting to compare the car to what was likely (in terms of price and market position) its closest competitor from rival Mercedes—the 280 SE 3.5 Coupe. Here the philosophical differences between the two companies could not be more clearly evident; while the two cars share certain similarities (very expensive German sports/luxury coupes made during the same period), the Mercedes feels like an entirely different type of car. Where the BMW can be driven like a sports car, the Mercedes demands a much more deliberate approach. Between them, there is no doubt where the two cars lie on the sports/luxury spectrum. That said, it must be noted there are several areas where the Mercedes clearly bests the lighter BMW. Both cars are quick, but the Mercedes achieves its speed with considerably less commotion then the CSL (or the plain CSi). Where the BMW demands effort and attention at the helm, the Mercedes (although not as fast), allows its driver to enjoy the car with less exertion.

A very large rear wing, a more traditional rear spoiler and front fender spats—these features proved enormously valuable in competition.

Compared with a standard 3.0CSi, the CSL is notably lighter at the front end, and feels like a smaller and more powerful car. Handling is more direct, with better feel through the leather-covered aluminum steering wheel. The car seems to brake with more urgency than the standard car, likely due to the difference in weight.

While dynamic differences between different versions of cars which are now over 20 years old could easily be obscured by differences in condition (or by modification from original specification), it appears that the differences between this coupe and the other 3.0CS/CSis I have driven were due largely to their original design. We note that it would be possible to recreate much of the feel and quality of the CSL through extensive modification to a 3.0CS or 3.0CSi, and many owners have done just that.

THE V12 COUPE

BMW built what will likely remain their single most desirable postwar vehicle for Hans Stuck Jr., who was among the company's most successful race drivers. That car was apparently a 3.0CSi or CSL fitted with a prototype 4.5-liter V-12 engine (as was later installed in the 750i sedan and 850i coupe). Very little is known of this car, or if it survives.

CHAPTER 5

Forging a Separate Path:
The M1 (E-26)

The M1 is immediately recognized as a very different sort of BMW. With a low-slung, mid-engined configuration, and with a sleek body crafted in fiberglass and designed by Giugiaro at Ital Design (Turin), the M1 is clearly and immediately a more sporting vehicle than any other road-going BMW.

BMW's sports car of the late 1970s represented at once a clean break from the company's traditional market and the clearest possible representation of their goals for the future. At its introduction, the M1 was perhaps unique in the world of high-performance sport cars in that it was functionally consistent with BMW's existing range of road cars. Unlike virtually all of its competitors, the M1 was and is an entirely useful and usable everyday vehicle.

The M1 was designed as more than BMW's flagship; the car was created primarily for competition (specifically Group 4). According to the company; "with the M1, the Bavarian Motor Works are not simply introducing a mid-engine sports car that is significantly different from the regular production models. Its concept is one that makes it unique even in the context of exclusive sports cars: the BMW M1 was planned and designed for racing. Then, from the racing car, a road car was developed."

The M1 in all its glory. BMW's only mid-engined sports car was supplied with a de-tuned version of the Motorsport Division's competition motor, putting out 277bhp.

That road car still stands as BMW's finest effort to date. The Motorsport Division supplied the M1 with a de-tuned version of their competition engine, complete with their own 4-valve-per-cylinder cross-flow head, Kugelfischer-Bosch mechanical fuel injection, dry-sump lubrication and 277bhp. Special attention was paid to the induction system; "the intake and exhaust tracts were laid out for maximum effectiveness, with little regard for complexity or cost. Air-fuel mixture flows through three double throttle pipes with six throttles (46mm diameter) into two intake tracts per cylinder of 26mm each. Two exhaust ports per cylinder, leading to an optimally-tuned exhaust system, provide efficient scavenging of the burned gases."

The M1 was provided with a chassis fully capable of putting that engine's power to efficient use. "In the road-going M1, the chassis is identical to that of the Group 4 model except for softer mounting of the moving parts and corresponded spring and damper settings. As is normal in race car design, suspension front and rear is by lateral links: more specifically, unequal-length lateral links, with light alloy wheel carriers, Bilstein gas-filled shock absorbers and concentric coil springs (adjustable for height) plus anti-roll bars." Tires are Pirelli P7s, size 205/55VR-16 front and 255/50VR-16 rear, mounted on special BMW Motorsport alloy wheels.

With the benefit of all that race-developed hardware, and with a curb weight of only 2867 pounds, the M1's performance was exceptional. The factory (whose figures are usually conservative), quoted 0-100 kilometers per hour acceleration of 5.6 seconds, and a top speed of 160 miles per hour. While that performance is roughly equal that produced by Porsche's 911 Turbo (the M1's closest competitor), the BMW was clearly superior to the Porsche in terms of handling of overall balance. In practice, any comparison between the two cars was probably not relevant; with only a handful of M1s produced, very few Porsche customers were likely to have even considered the possibility of the BMW sportscar.

If the M1 seemed to appear in an astonishingly fully developed state, it was probably because the

The most powerful of all the Schnitzer race cars, the BMW/Schnitzer M1 with twin turbos and 950bhp. Shown here driven by Hans-Joachim Stuck.

The M1 was designed as more than BMW's flagship; the car was created primarily for competition. Then, from the racing car, a road car was developed.

design combined well-proven (in competition) components with BMW's traditional preoccupation with careful engineering and build quality (together with a long gestation period). The factory realized early on that they were not well-configured to produce a limited-production exotic car. To fill the gap, BMW contacted a well-known manufacturer with a proposal to produce the M1 under contract.

At the time, BMW's decision to engage Lamborghini (the Italian supercar manufacturer) to build the M1 must have seemed entirely reasonable. BMW lacked not only the capacity, but also the experience to manufacture a mid-engine limited production car. In the end, Lamborghini disappointed. Fraught with problems of their own, including the ongoing prospect of insolvency, the Italian company was unable to fulfill their obligation—very little work on the M1 was completed at Lamborghini.

BMW returned the M1 project to Germany, relying upon Baur (the long-time manufacturer of

A total of 453 M1s were built, of which approximately 400 cars were for road use rather than competition.

factory-approved 2002 and 3-series-based convertibles) to complete development and assume production. In the end, the production M1s were exceptionally well-developed and superbly finished.

Outfitted according to the requirements of motorsport rather then the demands of fashion, a 15-year old M1 is today the equal of almost any modern sports car. A total of 453 M1s were built, of which approximately 400 cars were for road use rather than competition.

THE M1 TODAY

Even though the M1 will probably remain the most effective production road-going BMW ever built, the cars may ultimately be seen as a developmental deadend. If the M1 was the best possible assemblage of existing BMW parts, then (in evolutionary terms), it was nothing more than that. The car did not really set the stage for future projects—there have been no other mid-engined BMWs—and

will probably be remembered primarily as a magnificent break in the company's otherwise well-organized product history. Nonetheless, it is interesting to speculate on what would have resulted if BMW had continued the M1's development.

For those fortunate enough to have an M1 at their disposal today, the appeal of the car is undiminished. Even now, there are only a small handful of cars which can keep pace with a well-driven example. Compared with Italian exotic cars of the same period, the M1 will likely maintain its virtues much longer and with significantly less expense; having been designed and constructed as a BMW, M1s do not decay at anywhere near the rate of their contemporaries. During the height of the U.S. grey market (over the mid- to late-1980s), M1s were relatively popular among private importers. As such, while those cars are far from commonplace, examples *are* available both in Europe and in the U.S.

The chassis of the roadgoing M1 is identical to that of the Group 4 model except for softer mounting of the moving parts and corresponded spring and damper settings.

Following pages
Even though the design is now approaching 20 years old, it continues to look wonderful from any angle.

CHAPTER 6

The 5-Series Sedans (E-12, E-28 AND E-34)

THE E-12 5-SERIES; 1972-1981

The 1970s and early 1980s represented a period of remarkable sustained growth for BMW. It was during this period that the company's reputation in the United States became fully formed. For many American owners, BMW's original 5-series exemplified everything which BMWs were meant to represent; the cars were, by the standards of the time, fast, safe (both actively and passively), maneuverable and built to a standard which was even beyond their admittedly high price.

Among BMW enthusiasts, the E-12 5-series seems to inspire greater enthusiasm than its replacement (the E-28 5-series). The lasting appeal of the original 5-series is understandable; the car was superior to its competitors in much the same way that the earlier 2002 bested its rivals. A comparison between the 528i and the Mercedes 280E from the same period (both circa 1979-1981) clearly shows the BMW to be the more involving and capable of the two cars. Similar comparisons with the 5-series' other challengers (as conducted by numerous magazines) yielded similar results.

The U.S.-specification 1988 M5. Only produced for a single year for that market, the U.S. M5 was available only in black (usually with tan leather interior). Although a bit heavier and less powerful (by 30bhp) than the European-market M5, U.S. enthusiasts were grateful for each of the 1,235 examples imported.

Of particular interest is that BMW's E-12 5-series was available with a far wider range of engine alternatives than any of the company's previous models. During its lifespan, the first 5-series was actually available with every engine manufactured by the company; from the 100 horsepower 1.8 liter four to the 218 horsepower 3.5-liter six (and through 330 horsepower as turbocharged by Alpina).

The original E-12 5-series represented an excellent platform upon which to build even faster and higher-performance versions, a fact which both BMW Motorsport and Alpina were quick to realize. The results of their efforts are highly sought after today.

The Motorsport Specials (3.0, 3.3 and 3.5-liter)

From the early-1970s to the early-1980s, BMW Motorsport saw a fundamental change in mission. From a small enterprise responsible solely for the company's racing activities, Motorsport gradually came to stand for much of what BMW represented to the world at large. Motorsport began to more visibly advertise and promote its achievements, and to take a more active role in the development of road-going cars. By the early-1980s, Motorsport-developed components were evident on a large proportion of BMW's production cars.

Some of the most compelling designs from BMW Motorsport were never meant for the public. These cars were generally created for senior BMW executives, factory race drivers or very special customers. Because the 5-series was the company's primary offering during a period when BMW Motorsport was assuming a more important role within the company, that car was the beneficiary of much of Motorsport's early efforts. It appears that when the Motorsport division created a special car to the requirements of an important customer, that car was usually based on the early 5-series.

THE SIEFF 5-SERIES

In 1974, BMW Motorsport built a highly modified 5-series for the joint managing director of BMW Great Britain: the Sieff 5-series. Predating the announcement of a production large 6-cylinder 5-series by several years, the Sieff car utilized a 3.0 liter engine (essentially to CSL specification with a 305-degree camshaft). Also incorporated was an enhanced suspension, featuring specially-valved Bilstein shock absorbers and front and rear anti-sway bars. The car was specially prepared by Motorsport and can be assumed to have been virtually hand-built.

The Sieff 5-series is of particular interest because it is representative of a group of special cars which were built in very small numbers, and which are almost impossible to locate today. The Sieff car was known to have resided in England, and was offered for sale during 1990 at a price of U.K. pounds 8,000. At that price (and with car having a complete history), the buyer must have been very pleased with his purchase.

THE MOTORSPORT E-12 533i

In 1978, BMW took an intermediate (and historically unnoticed) step between the one-off Motorsport cars and the E-12 M535i—the first production-based motorsport road car (see below). For that year only, the company offered (through a Motorsport catalog dated May 1978) a factory conversion of the 525 and 528i models. This model (which apparently received no formal factory nomenclature, but which, for the sake of convenience, we will refer to as the E-12 533i), represented the first formal offering of a comprehensive Motorsport conversion to the public. Although this model has received essentially no attention in the literature, it clearly predates any other cataloged Motorsport production model.

The conversion transformed even the higher-performance 528i, bringing the finished cars to a significantly higher level of performance (not to mention providing their owners with a far greater measure of exclusivity). The most notable additions consisted of the company's 3.3-liter engine (as used in the 633 CSi and 733i) combined with the close-ratio (dog-leg) 5-speed gearbox (taken from the 635CSi) with a 25 percent limited-slip differential. As far as is generally known, the E-12 533i represented the only factory combination of these two components. Rated at 197 horsepower at 5,500 rpm, the 3.3-liter provided a meaningful performance increase compared with the regular production European-specification 528i.

Additional revisions to the Motorsport 533i included deeply contoured front seats (from either Recaro or a company called ASS), a special 380mm Motorsport steering wheel, and (unusually) mud flaps over the rear wheels, complete with large BMW insignias.

Externally, the 533i differed from conventional European-specification E-12 5-Series cars in several ways. Most noticeably, the cars were equipped with 14-inch diameter, 7-inch wide light alloy BBS rims and 195/70 VR 14 tires. These wheels deserve specific mention. Fitted with distinctive Motorsport center emblems, they do not appear to have been used on any previous factory car and only reappeared once on a production BMW—on the South African-manufactured version of the E-12 M535i (although it is believed that those wheels could be special ordered from the Motorsport division). BMW highest performance cars of that period—the 635 CSi and the M535i both made due with less extravagant 6.5x14-inch rims. At the rear, the E-12 533i was delivered with an unadorned rear decklid—no external badges gave onlookers any clue to the car's identity.

While specific production figures for these cars are unavailable, it is unlikely that any more than 100-200 cars with these specification were constructed during 1978. At least one of these cars is known to reside on the East Coast of the U.S.

THE MOTORSPORT E-12 533i;
DRIVING IMPRESSION

A drive in what is probably the only U.S.-resident 1978 Motorsport 533i demonstrates a considerable similarity with the later M535i. The gearboxes are identical, both in layout and gearing, and only the absence of the M535i's extra measure of high-end power really distinguishes them. As a collector car, the 533i is probably only slightly less desirable then a M535i—the 533i is even less common then the M535i, but the later car offers the ultimate E-12 factory specification and performance. As a car to use regularly, the 533i would offer essentially all of the advantages of a conventional 528i, but with significantly higher performance. The problem would be locating one.

THE FIRST M535i (E12)

If the M1 represented a departure from BMW's traditional business of building sports sedans, then the M535i was entirely consistent with the company's history. The fitting of progressively larger and more powerful engines into relatively light and agile cars has defined the company since the original 1500. Actually, BMW Motorsport's M535i is widely considered to be that division's second production vehicle (after the M1).

Even so, the M535i reflected a significant shift in BMW's approach to high-performance road cars. Previously, clients who wanted a roadgoing factory-produced example of BMW Motorsport's best efforts were generally turned away (unless they maintained some special connection to the factory). Now, after years of producing only very small numbers of road cars for important clients and company insiders, BMW Motorsport decided to sell cars to whomever could afford them (although still in very limited numbers). For BMW, the Motorsport connection was used to set the M535i apart from its production-based siblings. Its most obvious feature, indeed the raison d'etre for the car was its powerful, race-developed in-line 6-cylinder engine. According to the factory: "In its design and development, this 3.5-liter power unit is closely related to the various engines that power the BMW M1. Because both units have been developed out of the same engine, the extremely successful M49 racing engine which powered BMW's racing coupes from 1973 to 1976, developing no

One of the most interesting of all Motorsport cars; the original E-12-based M535i. BMW Motorsport supplied the cars with 3.5-liter, 218bhp engines and numerous other modifications. The car, while similar in appearance to the 528i, was very much faster.

less than 353 DIN kW (480hp) as a normally-aspiration engine and more than 588 DIN kW (800hp) in the turbocharged version."

As applied to the road-going M535i, the 3.5-liter engine developed not 800 horsepower or even 480 horsepower, but rather a very tractable and reliable 218 horsepower; identical to the same installation in the contemporary 635CSi. In almost all mechanical regards, the M535i was the identical twin to the much more common 635CSi. That similarity should not, however, in any way diminish the significance or desirability of the first-generation M535i—it was and remains a landmark in terms of understated performance.

As the first true production Motorsport car, the M535i was carefully positioned by BMW. The factory was clearly aware that although the car represented a continuation of the product philosophy

which had been developed since the original 1500, the M535i was a highly specialized product which required explanation. According to factory advertising literature: "The M535i represents a perfect symbiosis: First, it bears the name of a demanding manufacturer of standard production automobiles—a manufacturer which guarantees optimum production quality and a perfect finish. Second, it is the special product of a team of motor racing experts—a team that is able to combine its dedication and motor racing involvement with industrial resources, scientific know-how, and professional efficiency."

BMW's message here is plain; if a customer wanted a specially constructed high-performance car, but with the quality and practicality of a production BMW, their Motorsport Division stood ready to provide it.

THE E-12 M535i: DRIVING IMPRESSIONS

Over 15 years after the introduction of BMW's first production-based Motorsport road car, the E-12 M535i remains a pleasure to use as originally intended. With 218 horsepower available to motivate about 3000 pounds, and with the benefit of a precise, close-ratio 5-speed gearbox, the car is both fast and highly responsive. It is also dynamically superior to BMW's own first-generation 635 CSi of the same period (with which it shares an identical drivetrain). While not quite as low to the ground as its 6-series sibling, the E12 5-series is lighter, more rigid, easier to see out of, and has less overhang front and rear than the 635CSi. Those who have complained that the 6-series was seriously flawed due to deficiencies in those areas would have done well to sample the M535i (although the 635CSi was far from unsatisfactory in those regards, and was demonstrably superior to its competition).

The M535i has a precision and an eagerness which can only come from a powerful, relatively light car. Compared with the U.S.-specification 528i (itself an excellent car), the M535i is immediately set apart. While the two cars' basic platforms are essentially identical, the Motorsport car feels as though it was built for a different sort of customer.

A comparison with the earlier 3.0CSL (another Motorsport special, previously discussed) may be useful here. Despite significant differences in their conception and market positioning, and notwithstanding the nine years separating their introductions, the two have enough in common that the comparison seems worthwhile. Contemporary test reports indicate that the 3.0CSL and the M535i had almost identical performance (0-60 miles per hour in about 7.2 seconds, with a top speed of around 140 miles per hour), and that they (understandably) shared certain dynamic characteristics. An additional motivation for the comparison was the opportunity to drive both cars back-to-back. The 3.0CSL used was the same (3.2-liter) example described above.

Even allowing for the 7-year difference in their ages, the Motorsport 5-series seems a much more modern car than the lightweight coupe. The 5-series handles more securely—the greater rigidity of the M535i is immediately apparent, as is the fact that the later car enjoys a much more usable performance band. With the coupe, the performance is clearly there, but one must work to get at it.

Both the 5-series and the coupe demonstrate the superior engineering and construction which went into them. Despite obvious differences in their intended purposes, both cars provide an enormous amount of enjoyment.

REFURBISHMENT OF AN EARLY M535i

As with many other rare or unusual cars, the story of my involvement with a particular M535i is a somewhat complicated one. Given that there are perhaps only a dozen or so examples of the E-12 M535i in the U.S. (with no more coming in), the opportunity about 5 years ago to purchase one of these cars locally came as a surprise.

Upon first inspection, WBA47010004145134 (henceforth referred to as 5134) appeared to be in about average condition for its age and mileage. Painted in original but slightly faded Graphite metallic, and with the factory front and rear bumpers (rather than the spoiler and air dam setup), 5134 would have attracted no attention whatsoever from fellow motorists. The car was fitted with its original BBS alloy rims, Recaro seats, close-ratio 5-speed gearbox and 3.5-liter engine. The only deviation from stock appeared to be the replacement of the rare (and very difficult to find) M1-type steering-wheel with a regular 5-series item.

As reflected by its documentation, the car had been used by three previous owners. Originally purchased in Italy, 5134 was sold in the mid-1980s to an American family living there. Upon their return to the U.S. in 1988, they arranged to take the car back with them. That sort of arrangement was fairly uncommon by the late 1980s; most grey-market cars were imported either by companies specializing in that area, or by individuals who had never actually seen the car they were importing. Also, the original M535i was never a popular private import; most grey market cars were newer at the time of their importation. With only 1,806 E-12 versions produced, there were never very many available anyway.

After using the car in the States for several years, the family that imported it sold it to an individual who, while enthusiastic, appeared to have run the car on a very limited budget. With about two years of ownership and probably less then 2,000 miles, that owner sold the car to me. At that point (and with a broken odometer), we estimated that 4145134 had accumulated a total of approximately 70,000 to 80,000 miles.

While this M535i had not been pampered by a collector, neither had it suffered the abuses often heaped upon cars used everyday. 4145134 had spent most of its life garaged, and did not appear to have been in any major accident. Importantly, 4145134 came complete with its vital EPA and DOT paperwork. Without these items, even in view of the car's rarity, it would probably not have been purchased.

The only non-original component on the car seemed to be the steering wheel; the correct Motorsport wheel (also used on the M1) had been replaced with a standard item. One of the first purchases was an original M1/M535i steering wheel. That item, the location of which required almost a month's worth of transatlantic phone calls, came new in the factory wrapping.

As acquired, 4145134 required several items of immediate attention in order to make it roadworthy. Due to a prolonged period of inactivity, the car was given a complete service, with all fluids changed. All rubber hoses were replaced, and the valves were adjusted. All four tires were replaced with new rubber in the correct size. Upon inspection, a number of the car's major components were found to need repair or replacement. Age had clearly taken its toll on the original Bilstein shock absorbers. As the M535i was equipped with shocks especially valved for that car's suspension (and shared with no other model), correct units had to be sourced directly from Bilstein (at considerable expense). The brake system was completely overhauled, using all new components. All rubber bushings and mounts were replaced, and the driveshaft was refurbished.

Bodily, the M535i was generally sound, in that there was no serious or structural rust. However, the car did need a certain amount of attention. Both front fenders were replaced with original BMW factory items, and a small amount of rust perforation at the rear of the car (in front of the rear wheels) was repaired. Under the hood, the front suspension mounts were just beginning to rust (a common problem with most BMWs of this age). All compromised metal was removed, and new steel welded-in to a generally high standard.

The M535i's front bumper assembly had clearly been the victim of numerous parking lot encounters, and would need to be replaced. As the car came equipped with the standard chrome front bumper, rather than the optional front and rear spoiler package, I had intended to maintain that original specification. As I discovered that the cost of an original M535i front spoiler from BMW was less than the cost of the chrome bumper assembly, and given that this was a change which could be easily reversed, it was decided to go with the more functional front bumper.

After about two years of effort, the car is now fully roadworthy and in fine condition, and provides a great deal of enjoyment.

An early (circa 1977) Alpina-prepared 5-series, in this case the 230bhp 528 B2. This car was equipped with an Alpina fuel-injected 3-liter engine, and was capable of 0-100 kilometers per hour acceleration in 6.9 seconds. The 528 B2 predated Alpina's 3.5-liter cars.

THE 5-SERIES E-12 ALPINA CARS

While Alpina did not begin production of a cataloged 5-series car until December 1978 (with the remarkable B7 Turbo), the company's efforts with the new 5-series began almost immediately after it was introduced. Although those initial efforts generally involved individual work for specific customers (with various Alpina components chosen depending upon the requirements of the customer), by 1977 the company was preparing complete cars on a semi-production basis.

The early Alpina-prepared 5-series cars utilized components which had been well-proven in previous applications. Prior to the initiation of the more formal production models, Alpina offered two different packages based upon the E-12 sedans. As with previous Alpina cars, the focus here was on the engines; Alpina's two primary 6-cylinder motors were the 200bhp 2.8-liter B6 (as fitted later to Alpina's version of the original 3-series cars) and the 230bhp 3.0-liter B2 engine (as installed in the Alpina-modified early six-cylinder sedans and coupes).

Consistent with the company's desire to move toward the production of complete cars, rather then providing tuning work and performance components alone, these early 5-series cars were sold as complete automobiles. While it is likely that there was still considerable room for individual customers to dictate the final specification of their cars, Alpina now listed their 528 B6 and 528 B2 as distinct and complete models. With the exception of engines, the two cars were outfitted almost identically. Both were listed with 195/70 high-performance tires mounted on 7x14-inch Alpina light-alloy rims, both were fitted with special Alpina-Bilstein suspension systems and both were sold with front spoilers and complete Alpina interior kits. For those who wanted this same package applied to a more sporting body style, essentially all components fitted to the B2 version were available for the then-new 6-series coupe.

While later versions of the E-12 sedan offered larger displacement engines and even more performance, the 528 B6 and B2 models were paragons of performance by the standards of the mid-1970s. Alpina (who were usually completely reliable on these issues) listed acceleration figures from 0-100 kilometers per hour for the B6 of 7.6

seconds, and for the B2 of only 6.9 seconds. Top speeds were listed at 212 kilometers per hour for the B6 and 228 kilometers per hour for the B2. It is worth noting that the performance figures for the B2 indicate that the car would have been fully competitive with contemporary sports cars from Porsche and Ferrari.

Alpina continued to offer a naturally aspirated version of the E-12 5-series even after the release of their turbo-charged models. From late 1981, the B9 was available with a 245hp version of the 3.5l engine, and with a full complement of Alpina equipment as with the B6 and B2 models.

THE B7, B7S TURBO

THE ALPINA B7 TURBO

Alpina's first conversion based upon BMW's original 5-series went well beyond any factory production offering. Where BMW cautiously offered first 197 horsepower by their 3.3-liter engine, then 218 horsepower from their 3.5-liter, Alpina stepped forward with no less than an expertly turbocharged 3.0-liter conversion offering 300 horsepower. This car, made available from December 1978, was called the Alpina B7 and was, in all probability, the fastest sedan in the world.

These turbocharged Alpina conversions were the ultimate examples of the E-12 5-series cars. However, the B7s sold in such small numbers that they tend to be overlooked by BMW enthusiasts (total production equaled just 149 B7 Turbos and 60 B7S Turbos). Certainly their specifications suggest that they deserve greater attention; the cars were lavishly equipped with every performance item at Alpina's well-stocked disposal. Little attention seems to have been paid to cost; the final version carried a price of DM 75,000 in Germany, at a time when a fully-equipped (from BMW) 528i sold for less then half that amount.

An examination of an original B7 Turbo reveals the extent to which these cars were recreated by Alpina. Exterior changes were relatively minor (compared with the fundamental engineering changes made to the cars). B7s received Alpina's customary "Deco" striping, along with an Alpina front air dam and rear spoiler. Alpina's trademark alloy wheels (here at 16-inch diameter) were fitted. Additionally, the car sits somewhat lower than would an unmodified BMW 5-series, due to the revised suspension. It is only when the car is viewed in detail that the range of Alpina's work becomes evident. At the rear, Alpina fitted a proprietary differential cooler to handle the greater stresses which would likely be inflicted upon that component. The battery has been moved to the trunk for better weight distribution (under a specially made holder). Wherever you look on the car, changes have been made to improve the basic design. Moreover, those changes have clearly been accomplished with an enormous degree of craftsmanship and care.

In their March 1979 issue, *Road & Track* tested an Alpina B7 Turbo (in Europe). While timing runs were not conducted, the testers found no reason to doubt Alpina's claims of 0-60 miles per hour in 5.9 seconds, and a top speed of 155 miles per hour. The magazine quoted a price for the Alpina B7 of 59,920 DM or approximately $31,500 at the then current exchange rate. At that price (which would not have included transport or federalization expenses), the car cost about twice the price of a U.S.-specification 528i.

THE ALPINA E-12 B7S TURBO

From the mid-1970s to early 1980s, Alpina had produced some of their most effective cars using the original 5-series. The company's final effort

This second-series (E-28) M535i has a 3.5 liter fuel injection engine (160kW/218bhp).

based on the E-12 platform represented a magnificent example of their abilities.

For the last of the Alpina E-12 cars, the company created a limited edition of only 60 cars. Produced for six months (from November 1981 to May 1982), these cars were distinguished by their brilliant special Sapphire Blue metallic paint with contrasting gold Alpina stripes ("Sonderfarbe dunkelsaphireblau metallic mit Goldsteifen auf Interieur abgestimmt"). Alpina loaded these vehicles with almost every performance and luxury component from their substantial catalog. The B7S was equipped with the company's most potent engine; a 330 horsepower version of their turbocharged 3.5-liter powerplant.

In terms of scarcity and desirability, there is very little to compare with the E-12 Alpina B7/B7S Turbos. With a total production of only 209 over a four year period, there are almost none to go around. Additionally, the concept of a vehicle with standard-setting levels of power and performance in a relatively conservative shell (dating back to 1972) has a certain durable appeal.

All of the later Alpina cars can be identified as genuine by their separate chassis number/identification badges located on the dashboard immediately in front of the front passenger. As with the earlier cars, however, documentation remains critically important in determining both the provenance and the configuration of a particular Alpina vehicle. Given both the willingness of Alpina to indulge in wishes of specific clients (and to deviate from their standard specifications) and also the ease with which these cars could be modified over time, the confirmation provided by complete documentation becomes invaluable.

DRIVING IMPRESSION:
THE 5-SERIES B7 TURBO

In the course of preparing this book, we were fortunate enough to have access to an original E-12 Alpina B7 Turbo. This car (probably one of no more than two or three in the U.S., and believed to be the only one on the East Coast) was specially prepared by Alpina to conform with the specific wishes of a certain customer. Unlike almost all other such cars, this B7 was equipped with a leather, rather than cloth interior. Also, the traditional Alpina "Deco" stripes were requested deleted from this car when ordered. In all other respects, the car is very much as it was originally delivered by the Alpina factory, and should provide a fair representation of the class. What is most surprising about the car is its relatively sedate appearance (especially without Alpina's trademark stripes).

Upon further inspection, the extent to which the B7 was not just a modified BMW, but rather an entirely re-engineered and remanufactured car becomes evident. Indeed, both the quantity and the quality of the Alpina equipment fitted to the car is remarkable. Inside, deeply-contoured seats (manufactured to Alpina's specifications by Scheel) replaced the standard 5-series items. All instruments have been replaced with special Alpina gauges, recalibrated and featuring very serious-looking bright red indicators. Supplemental instrumentation with gauges for turbo boost level, oil pressure and oil temperature has been incorporated into a custom-built binnacle located on top of the dashboard and angled towards the driver. Other immediately apparent Alpina equipment includes the special leather covered steering wheel, the shift knob, a left-foot dead pedal and the large Alpina variable boost control located between the two front seats.

For all of the obvious equipment differences between the B7 and BMW's production 5-series cars, it is only upon driving this Alpina that it is revealed for what it is: a very specialized, essentially hand-built high-performance car. While any comparison with a U.S.-specification 530i or 528i (or, for that matter, a European-specification 528i) would be entirely unfair, it is immediately apparent that the B7 is very different from even an E-12 M535i (the BMW factory's most potent production effort on the same chassis). Surprisingly, low-end torque seems at least as strong as in the M535i, the combination of a smaller displacement (3.0 liters against 3.5 for the M535i) together with the lower compression ratio made necessary by the forced induction system (now at 7.0 to 1) would normally lead to relatively mild low-rpm performance. I judged the B7s performance below 3,000rpm to be roughly the equal of the M535i. However, and as with almost all turbocharged applications, the real benefits of the system are made apparent at higher revs. Here, the B7 is absolutely astonishing. Even with the adjustable boost knob set near the low-end of its range, the car accelerates at an unbelievable rate. Contemporary road tests produced 0-60 miles per hour times of approxi-

Unlike the earlier version, the second-series (E-28) M535i cars were essentially specially-equipped 535is, rather than ground-up Motorsport vehicles.

mately 5.9 seconds—blistering fast even by modern standards. Top speed was quoted by Alpina at 155 miles per hour. Circa 1980, only a handful of the fastest and most expensive production cars (notably from Italy) would have been at all competitive with the Alpina B7.

Perhaps as surprising as the B7's enormous power and performance is its tractability. For all the car's abilities, it remains a usable and practical car. With the turbo boost knob turned to its lowest (most restrictive) setting, and avoiding revs much over 3500rpm, the car could almost pass as a stock 528i (although the firmer ride and razor-sharp handling would be hard to overlook). When driven with purpose, however, the B7's purpose becomes clear—there are very few sedans in the world (and certainly none of this vintage) which could keep pace with a well-driven example.

THE SECOND GENERATION 5-SERIES (E-28) CARS

After 10 years of production, the E-12 5-series was still considered a class-leading sports sedan. The market, however, demands continual new product cycles, and BMW's competitors were certainly

The original M5. While lacking any obvious signs as to the work performed by BMW's Motorsport Division, the M5 was substantially modified in almost all respects. The European-market M5 came equipped with a 24-valve, 3.5 liter 286bhp engine.

not standing still. The company was here presented with a dilemma: how to balance the more traditional expectations of their customer base against the trend towards more aggressively aerodynamic styling. In retrospect, it seems clear that BMW made too conservative a choice; the E-28 5-series (introduced for the 1982 model year) incorporated a number of subtle improvements over the E-12, but bore an uncomfortably close resemblance to the much earlier E-3 cars (the Bavaria/3.0Si). Aesthetically, the car suffered by comparison with its predecessor; immediately recognizable as a car designed by engineers, rather then stylists, the original 5-series had a certain timeless appeal. Deprived of the E-12's more appealing curves, the resulting E-28 appeared unnecessarily boxy.

THE SECOND M535i (E-28)

In 1979, the idea of equipping the mid-size 5-Series with BMW's largest and most powerful engine was probably seen as an extravagance; the factory certainly did not see these cars as mass-market products, and only a very limited number were ever built. By 1984, the idea had become not only more familiar, but also a competitive necessity. Competition from other manufac-

turers (such as Mercedes with their large V-8 engined cars) compelled BMW to follow suit. Like the original 5-series/3.5-liter engine combination, the second-generation car was also called the M535i. Unlike the original M535i, the second-generation M535i was not really a Motorsport product. Where the E-12 car was a "special version developed and manufactured by BMW Motorsport GmbH," the E-28 M535i car was only the top-of-the-range 5-Series. By the time of its introduction, the 3.5-liter engine installed in the E-28 M535i was used communally throughout the BMW range (in the 635CSi, the 735i and even the regular 535i).

Issues such as the availability of an automatic transmission, the lack of any special Motorsport components and the fact that the cars were built on the regular factory production line (rather than by the Motorsport division) further differentiated the second generation M535i from its more desirable E-12 predecessor.

Given that they are of recent vintage, many E-28 M535is survive in good condition. As a relatively inexpensive alternative to other E-28 5-series cars (the 528e, 528i etc.), they represent an interesting choice.

For American buyers not able to afford the considerable price of the M5 (or not needing that car's very high level of performance), BMW offered a U.S.-specification car very similar to the European-market M535i. This car, called the 535is, offered a drivetrain identical to the U.S. 535i. As compensation BMW provided U.S. customers with a more aggressive suspension (lower and stiffer), front and rear spoilers

As with the E-28 M535i, the 535is was available with both 5-speed and automatic transmissions. Although it was not really a factory high-performance version (neither was the second M535i), it introduced many to the sporting virtues of a properly equipped BMW.

THE FIRST M5: TAKING THE CONCEPT ONE STEP FURTHER

When BMW replaced their popular E-12 5-Series in 1981, they did so at a time when aerodynamics were just beginning to play an active role in vehicle design. Given the multi-year lead-times associated with the production of a new car from BMW, it is understandable that they chose to move ahead conservatively. In retrospect, the company moved too cautiously. The resulting platform (called the E-28) was so similar to its predecessor that many people were unable to distinguish the two. While superior in several ways to the E-12 cars, this new 5-Series did not represent the sort of major improvement that customers had come to expect with new models from BMW. Especially in view of the relatively long life of the E-12, the E-28 was perhaps a smaller step forward than usual for the company.

In fact, the overall design of the car may even be seen as retrograde; there is more than a passing resemblance to the older E-3 class sedans (which dated from 1968).

Today, the E-28 5-Series is considered less desirable than similarly configured E-12 cars. There was, however, one E-28 derivation which went considerably beyond any factory production effort with the earlier chassis, and which was probably the best standard BMW of the period—the M5.

With the introduction of the M635CSi, and with the knowledge that BMW had installed that same 24-valve engine in the previous E-12 5-series (if only for test purposes), speculation began as to its installation in the new sedan.

When the M5 did arrive (in Europe for 1985), no one was disappointed. Unlike the production E-28 M535i, the new M5 had no aggressive spoil-

BMW enthusiasts in the U.S. had to wait until three years after the M5's introduction to the European market (the 1988 model year) to sample the M5.

ers or air dams suggesting its performance potential. Rather, the car was positioned as the ultimate "Q-ship," with nothing to give away the fact that this was the fastest production BMW (short of the M1) ever made.

Much of the M5's appeal came from the fact that it appeared to be nothing more than a lower-end 5-series sedan. Nothing could have been further from the truth—according to the factory; "The M5 is available on individual order as a special model from Motorsport GmnH. The M5 combines the understated styling and sedan practicality of the BMW 5-series with all the potency and luxury BMW Motorsport knows how to build into a car." The M5's potency came from the same 3.5-liter, 24-valve dual-overhead cam engine as fitted to the M635CSi. With 286 horsepower, and as installed in the lighter 5-series, the M5 proved to be a remarkable performer; acceleration from 0-100 kilometers per hour was achieved in only 6.5 seconds, with the car reaching a top speed of over 150 miles per hour. The European-specification M5 was the least showy, highest-performance sedan available during the mid- to late-1980s, and was very highly regarded by those fortunate to have access to one.

In the U.S., BMW enthusiasts had to wait until three years after the M5's introduction to the European market (the 1988 model year) to sample the M5. Much to the delight of American BMW enthusiasts, the company did decide to import the car for the last year of E-28 production. Given the company's relatively indifferent attitude towards the U.S. high-performance market (in the mid-1980s), this decision needs to be viewed within the context of overall corporate strategy. By 1985, the effect of the grey market was becoming more pronounced for American BMW dealers; where privately imported cars had historically accounted for only the smallest fraction of total imports, they were taking noticeable market share away from the BMW corporate dealer network. The reason for this was relatively simple; with the dollar-to-German mark relationship favoring the dollar by a significant margin (in terms of purchasing power parity), U.S. enthusiasts found that they could bring over more desirable European versions of the cars they wanted at substantial cost savings relative to their U.S.-specification equivalents.

BMW North America made several changes to the E-28 M5, most of which served to bring it into conformity with U.S. safety and emission standards (as with the rest of the E-28 range). As with the rest of the 5-series range, U.S.-specification M5s were fitted with larger and heavier bumpers front and rear, and with additional side reflectors (neither of which improved the car's overall appearance).

U.S. M5s were, on the whole, more lavishly outfitted than their European equivalents, but with less choice available to the purchaser. Actually, U.S. M5 buyers had no choice whatsoever with respect to the specifications of their cars. All U.S.-bound M5s were supplied with identical black paint work (which extended to areas such as window moldings and bumpers—parts that were usually chromed—and with luxurious tan leather interiors. It has been suggested that a very small

The M5 was capable of accelerating from 0-60 miles per hour in about 6.2 seconds.

number of cars (perhaps a dozen) were fitted with black, rather than tan interiors.

While the U.S. version of BMW's fastest-ever sedan was somewhat diminished from the European-specification car (horsepower was down from 286 to 256, weight was up to 3,420 pounds from 3,153 pounds), it still came as a revelation to the American market. With acceleration from 0-60 in only 6.7 seconds (about 0.5 seconds slower than the European-specification car) it is unlikely that U.S. drivers noticed any missing horsepower. Especially compared with previous U.S.-specification 5-series, it was clear that BMW had become more serious about addressing the demands of performance-oriented drivers within that market.

An interesting story (one which is more a commentary on the American legal system than on BMW) revolved around the U.S. version of the E-28 M5. Because the factory originally planned that only 500 copies of their highest-performance 5-series would be imported into the U.S., advertisements made mention of that fact in describing the car. When it later turned out that more than the original 500 cars were built for the U.S. (in fact 1,235 cars were imported by the end of the production run), several customers organized a class-action lawsuit against BMW claiming false advertising. The case was eventually settled, with every U.S. M5 purchaser given a credit towards the purchase of a new BMW.

The first-generation M5 provided both U.S. and European drivers with more performance

The M5 is still one of the most desirable of all BMWs.

Alpina's 5-series-based B9 3.5.

The much-modified 3.5-liter sedan provided a significant increase in performance compared with the 535i on which it was based.

Only an M5 or Alpina's own B7 Turbo would have been faster than the 5-series-based B9 3.5.

Although significantly more expensive than the standard model upon which it was based, the B9 3.5 was competitively priced with cars offering similar performance.

than had been previously available in a conservatively-dressed sedan. As with several previous models from BMW, the M5 again raised the standard for sports sedans.

THE E-28 5-SERIES ALPINA CARS

By 1982, Alpina was recognized as a fully independent automobile manufacturer. The company was now a larger and more professionally-run organization, and was able to smoothly integrate BMW's new 5-series into their product range. While there was never any real question that Alpina versions of the E-28 cars would be produced, this integration was no doubt made easier by the fact that the car was so similar to it's (E-12) predecessor.

Alpina was actually somewhat slow to embrace the new 5-series platform. Company records indicate that the first Alpina E-28 car was not produced until January 1983, over a year after the standard factory cars were made available to the public. Moreover, Alpina vehicles based upon the earlier 5-series were apparently produced until August 1983. The assumption here is that given Alpina's limited production and the somewhat retrograde nature of the newer car's styling, the company did not see the need to immediately change their E-12-based vehicles over to E-28 specification.

Alpina's first conversion to the E-28 took the form of their standard B9: a package well-proven on the earlier 5-series. As before, the Alpina version provided 245 horsepower from the familiar 3.5-liter 6-cylinder engine.

The company's next offering on the second-generation 5-series platform (not available until April 1984) was their awe-inspiring B7 Turbo. It is interesting to note that, although the E-28 version of the B7 Turbo utilized the larger 3.5-liter engine (as with the previous B7S Turbos installed in both the 5- and 6-series cars), the newer 5-series had only 300 horsepower, not the 330 horsepower available in either the earlier 5-series or the 6-series.

THE E-28 5-SERIES TUNER CARS:
OTHER EFFORTS
THE HARTAGE H5S

By the mid-1980s, Hartage had established a successful operation selling high-performance BMW parts and tuning cars for customers. What the company had not yet done was to make a business building complete cars. With the E-28 5-series (and concurrently with the E-30 3-series), Hartage made a more concerted effort to compete directly with Alpina in selling finished cars.

With the introduction of the H5S in 1985, Hartage offered a direct competitor to both Alpina's B9 and BMW's own M535i. Fitted with most of the company's specialized high-performance components, the Hartage car was powered by a 3,453cc engine brought up to 240bhp (compared with BMW's 218bhp) through the utilization of traditional tuning techniques.

In terms of performance, the H5S is closely comparable to Alpina's E28 B9 and BMW's second-generation M535i. The sprint from 0-60 miles per hour was achieved in 6.9 seconds, with 100 miles per hour coming up in 17.3 seconds. Hartage claimed a top speed of 144 miles per hour, although contemporary road tests achieved a bit less.

While it might be difficult to define what would constitute an original H5S (given the degree of flexibility given to the purchaser), a car prepared by Hartage with all of the basic H5S equipment (and with documentation to that effect) would certainly qualify. It appears that Hartage's standards of engineering and construction were fully as high as BMW's own. From a collectibility standpoint, the Hartage H5S would take a back seat to either an Alpina B7 Turbo or an M5, but would be on par with an Alpina B9 or an M535i (assuming the car had been prepared by Hartage when new).

BMW's second-generation (E-34) M5. Seen here in its original form (prior to a series of upgrades including different rims), the new M5 provided both greater comfort and higher performance than the E-28 version.

THE SCHNITZER S5

Schniter's E-28 528i-based S5 was one of the company's few formally catalogued production cars. As with similar conversions from Alpina and Hartage, Schnitzer utilized a specially tuned version of BMW's 3.5-liter 6-cylinder engine. With the benefit of Schnitzer's special components, the S5 engine produced 245bhp—enabling the car to accelerate from 0-100 kilometers per hour in 6.9 seconds, and to reach a top speed of about 240 kilometers per hour. As with the Alpina and Hartage cars, the S5 was a complete conversion; incorporating upgraded suspension, brakes, 16 inch BBS alloy wheels and associated ancillary equipment.

THE THIRD-GENERATION
(E-34) 5-SERIES CARS

If the second iteration of their mainstay 5-series was considered too conservative at the time of its introduction, BMW's third-generation 5-series had no such problem. The new 5-series (introduced in 1989), represented a leap forward in design. While the E-28 was still competitive in terms of overall quality and engineering, the E-34 provided a much more modern platform for many of the same mechanical components.

THE M5 (E-34)

Such had been the enormous public enthusiasm for the original M5, that there was never any doubt

BMW's U.S. replacement for the M5, the 540i Sport combined the M5's suspension, brakes, wheels and bodywork with the company's 4.0-liter V-8 engine.

that the 1988 E-34 chassis would receive the full Motorsport treatment. The car was introduced in 1989 to almost unanimously enthusiastic reviews. While the second generation M5 was both larger and heavier than the E-28 5-series, it benefited both from the considerably more advanced E-34 platform, and also from the ongoing development work on the 6-cylinder Motorsport engine. While the basic architecture of the 24-valve six-cylinder engine remained the same, displacement was increased slightly—from 3453cc to 3535cc. Additionally, compression now rose from 9.8:1 to 10.0:1, and significant work was done to the intake system. Those changes allowed for a meaningful increase in power; where the original M5 had been provided with 256bhp in U.S. trim and 282bhp in Europe, the new (U.S.-specification) M5 was now good for 310bhp.

As with the rest of the E-34 range, the M5 provided significant advances in torsional rigidity, allowing the car to more fully utilize the upgraded Motorsport powerplant. While weight had risen as

well (now at 3,846 for the U.S-specification car), performance was even better than before. The new M5 proved capable of acceleration from 0-60 miles per hour in only 5.6 seconds, and went on to an (electronically-limited) top speed of 155 miles per hour.

The E-34 M5 was only available in the U.S. market from model years 1991-1993, although the car was available in Europe through the end of E-34 production. For the U.S. market only, BMW provided a special run of 200 540i Sport cars during the 1996 model year. That car combined the M5's chassis components with the (later) 4.0-liter V-8 engine.

ALPINA'S THIRD-GENERATION (E-34) 5 SERIES CARS

While the higher equipment levels and elevated market position of BMW's third-generation 5-series fit well with Alpina's move towards more expensive and fully-developed automobiles, this notably larger and heavier car presented them with certain challenges. Chief among those was reconciling the size of the new car with the level of performance to which the company's customers had grown accustomed. Alpina's response was to offer more sophisticated engineering and even more powerful engines. While the company offered a version of the E-32 with their standard tuning package (the regular B10 with 254bhp, of which 572 units were produced), Alpina now turned to more sophisticated techniques for their most powerful 5-series.

THE ALPINA 5-SERIES B10 BITURBO

By the later 1980s, Alpina's relationship with BMW had evolved such that the two companies worked together during the development of new models. As a result, Alpina was able to introduce their most serious effort based on the third-generation 5-series shortly after the model's release in 1989. The company's B10 Biturbo was introduced in that same year, with the first car completed in August 1989. The Biturbo benefited significantly from BMW's re-engineering of the basic platform. The E-32 5-series was significantly more rigid and more aerodynamic than its predecessor, and allowed Alpina to build in even higher levels of performance.

While similar in concept to Alpina's earlier B7 turbocharged engines, the B10 Biturbo (as its name indicates) utilized a pair of smaller and lighter turbochargers—enabling the engine to

BMW's second-generation M5, which benefited from all of the work that went into the E-34 platform. A more sophisticated car than the original M5, it was both more comfortable and faster than its predecessor.

Almost as fast as the M5 (production of which had ceased in 1994 for the U.S. market), the 1996 540i Sport was considered by some better suited to U.S. driving conditions.

build boost more quickly. So equipped, and fully modified by Alpina for greater power, the Biturbo developed a remarkable 360bhp from its (un-changed) 3430cc displacement. Faster even than BMW's own second-generation M5, the Alpina car was capable of accelerating from 0-60 miles per hour in about 5.0 seconds, and was able to reach a top speed of approximately 180 miles per hour. Contemporary testers remarked on the car's extra-ordinary stability and comfort, even at speeds well over 150 miles per hour.

With 507 5-series cars built in total, the B10 Biturbo represented a significant base of business for Alpina. It is not believed that any Biturbos were imported into the U.S.

THE HARTAGE 12-CYLINDER 5-SERIES

With regard to the mating of larger engines with smaller cars, the unwritten rule among BMW tuners has always been "if it can be made to fit, try it out." With that in mind, it was inevitable that someone would attempt to install the 5.0-liter V-12 from the 750i into the E-32 body. Hartage may not have been the first to try, but they at least seem to have built more of these interesting hybrids than anyone else.

The 540i Sport interior.

Alpina's B10 Biturbo motor undergoing bench testing. As fitted to their E-34 5-series-based sedan, this engine provided outstanding performance and flexibility. Maximum power of 360bhp is produced.

Right
The Alpina B10 Bi-Turbo. With twin turbochargers and 360bhp, this is Alpina's most powerful 5-series-based car. The B10 Bi-Turbo is capable of a top speed in excess of 180 miles per hour. *Alpina Automobile Meisterwerke catalog*

Below
The 5-series-based Alpina B10 Bi-Turbo. 360bhp, 0-100 kilometers per hour acceleration in 6.3 seconds and a top speed of 180 miles per hour.

With BMW now offering their V-8 engine in the 5-series sedan, Alpina has developed a higher-performance version of that same car. The Alpina B10 4.0 is based on the 4.0-liter 540i, but with additional tuning to provide 315bhp at 5,800rpm. *Alpina Automobile Meisterwerke catalog*

CHAPTER 7

The 3-Series Cars:
High-Performance in a Small Package

THE SUCCESSOR TO THE 2002:
THE FIRST 3-SERIES (E-21)

After 10 years and the sale of almost 750,000 cars, BMW was justifiably slow to replace their successful and profitable 2002 with a newer model. In fuel-injected tii form, the 2002 represented the ultimate development of the platform which helped produce BMW's postwar recovery. By the mid-1970s, the car had been refined and improved to the point where it was difficult to fault, and had gained an enormously enthusiastic following (which continues to this day). The 2002's successor, the E-21 3-series, was conceived with a different purpose than its predecessor. Where the 2002 was meant to provide basic transportation for an enthusiastic owner (who probably cared very little about automotive styling) the 320i was designed to appeal to a new group of BMW owners.

As is true of many early BMW's compared with the later cars, the 2002 was and is a more visceral device; it has inspired greater emotion because its intent is more explicit. It seems easier to generate enthusiasm for the 2002 than for the first-generation 3-series cars. That said, the enduring appeal of the 2002 should in no way diminish the virtues of the E-21 3-series. The (completely standard) U.S.-specification 1983 320i which served as my primary transportation for about one year was incredibly

An Alpina-prepared Group A M3 at speed in 1987.

The first-generation (E-21) 3-series, seen here in the form of the six-cylinder, 143bhp 323i. While BMW themselves did not offer a true high-performance version of the 3-series until the later E-30 cars, the 323i was a reasonably quick car.

well-built, relentlessly durable, and was utterly predictable in its handling. The principal vice of these early 3-series was considered to be a certain viciousness over wet or icy roads, a reputation which was wholly accurate.

The early 3-series was extremely successful in expanding the appeal of the small BMW to a far larger audience. The car's softer, more pleasing lines (to a late-1970s/early-1980s aesthetic) combined with a notably higher level of equipment than was available in the 2002 appealed to many who might have thought that the 2002 was a bit spartan.

While the absolute performance capabilities of the cars discussed here are obviously important, we have made an effort to view them against their contemporaries. Although the 323i (BMW's highest-performance version of the E-21 3-Series) was certainly as quick as the 2002tii, we have not included any factory-production version of the first-generation 3-series in this discussion. That the two cars are today evenly-matched in terms of acceleration and top speed is easy to observe. By the standards of the time (1971) however, the 2002tii represented a significant advancement past competing sports sedans. While the 323i was a quick and satisfying car, unlike its predecessor, it was not the definitive product in its class.

Comparing the two today, the earlier car is at once both less refined and more involving; there is

a directness and immediacy to the 2002tii (due largely to its light weight and the responsiveness of its mechanical fuel-injection system) which is not matched by its successor. Although produced in huge numbers (for BMW), and while a significant success in the market, the replacement for the 2002 was less than satisfactory for some enthusiasts. Nonetheless, the 3-series cars were generally very good by the standards of the time. Given that those cars were the smallest and lightest made by BMW during their production, it was inevitable that improving their performance would be the object of great attention.

THE HIGH PERFORMANCE 4-CYLINDER 3 SERIES CARS

In the U.S., the 320i (the only version made available) did little to enrich BMW's performance image. With a curb weight of 2,400 pounds, and with the 2.0 liter (1.8 liter from 1980) engine providing an emaciated 100 horsepower, the car could only manage 0-60 miles per hour in about 11.0 seconds. More to the point, and perhaps for the first time in the company's postwar history, the U.S.-specification 320i was no faster nor a more capable handler than far less expensive competition from other companies. What had distinguished the 2002 in the U.S. was not its performance in an absolute sense, but rather that it was demonstrably superior to its contemporaries (at no great price premium). The U.S. 320i, hindered by a less favorable relationship between the U.S. dollar and the German mark, lost that advantage.

In the struggle to regain it (often at considerable cost), some of these cars did serve as the basis for conversions by Alpina, Hartage and Schnitzer. While cars which were originally delivered as U.S.-specification vehicles could not be considered factory efforts, many of them were exceptionally well-executed.

Although none of the BMW factory E-21 4-cylinder cars could be classified as high-performance cars (and we are aware of no factory specials based upon the 4-cylinder E-21 platform), some European-market cars were undoubtedly fitted with various Motorsport components—either by the factory or by enthusiastic dealers. In the U.S., BMW did offer an optional 320i Sport Package, consisting of a more aggressive suspension, BBS rims, Recaro seats and a sports steering wheel. U.S. enthusiasts set upon owning a U.S.-specification (non-grey market) E-21 should certainly seek out those cars so equipped.

THE LARGE-ENGINE E-21 3-SERIES CARS

As discussed above, the combination of BMWs largest engine in their smallest car was a concept which began with the 2002 (essentially the 1600 with BMW's 2-liter motor). The fundamental appeal of that idea has proved so enduring that enthusiasts continued to pursue it even after the physics of such an arrangement became more challenging. While the first transplant of the large 6-cylinder engine in the early 3-series body is impossible to document, subsequent conversions by

Right
Today, a well-preserved E-21 Alpina would be entirely suited either for daily driving or weekend enjoyment.

Two views of early Alpina-prepared E-21 3-series cars (circa 1977).

Alpina and other tuners (using engines displacing 2.8, 3.0, 3.3 and 3.5 liters) met with considerable success from 1977 to 1983.

While most histories disclaim BMW's direct involvement with the marriage of their largest engine to the 3-series, the company did produce such a car themselves. BMW South Africa offered a machine called the 333i (3.3 liter six cylinder in an E-30 body). This vehicle, which was conceived by BMW's South African subsidiary and manufactured in that country, utilized several chassis components from Alpina's similar big-six engined car. The resulting vehicle stands as one of the most interesting factory-produced cars of the period.

THE ALPINA E-21 3-SERIES CARS

As with the 5- and 6-series car, Alpina produced a considerable body of work based on BMW's new 3-series before offering a formal cataloged model. Most of that work for the early 3-series cars focused on the well-proved 4-cylinder engine. As fitted to the first generation 3-series, Alpina offered a choice of at least four different engines; the A1/3 (with 120bhp), the A2/3 (with 150bhp), the A4/3 (with 160bhp) and the A4S/3 (with 170bhp). These engines were broadly similar to earlier versions fitted to 02 series cars, with only small evolutionary changes. Alpina four-cylinder engines for 3-series cars were identified by their "/3" designations. It should be noted that while the A4S/3 is listed as an available option in contemporary Alpina literature, there is no record of examples of that engine being installed in 3-series cars. Production figures *are* available for the A2/3 (113 cars were fitted with those engines between July 1975 and September 1978), and for the A4/3 (with 120 cars produced between May 1976 and May 1986). No production totals are available for E-21 cars fitted with A1/3 engines, and it seems unlikely that many were built.

It should be noted that no formal separate Alpina model was based upon the 4-cylinder car, and that the cars discussed above could be ordered with engine modifications only. Despite the fact that those cars were not cataloged models, it is likely that most E-21 four-cylinder Alpina-built cars *were* fully equipped as delivered.

It is interesting to note that Alpina were themselves fitting an A4 engine to an E-21 3-series car as

late as 1986—three years after BMW's production of that car had ended. The duration between that car's original production by BMW and its modification by Alpina reflects the difference between cars *modified* by Alpina (which could be performed at any time during those cars' lives), and cars *produced* by Alpina. The production of separate models would only be performed using brand new cars.

While BMW produced a substantial range and volume of performance equipment for the 4-cylinder E-21 and for the small 6-cylinder version, Alpina produced only a single cataloged model based upon the smaller-engine 6-cylinder E-21 (the popular C1). The C1 provided lively performance from its 2.3-liter, 170 horsepower engine—fully the equal of the exotic four-cylinder from their earlier A4/3, but with considerably greater refinement. Between April 1980 and July 1983, Alpina produced 462 examples of their E-21-based C1.

In four-cylinder form, the E-21 3-series was never considered a fast car. While BMW's installation of their small (2.3 liter) six-cylinder engine went a long way in terms of improving performance, the 3-series continued to be viewed as less-agile and not as quick in day-to-day driving as its 2002 predecessor.

From November 1978, Alpina's B6 redressed any performance complaints about the 3-series from enthusiastic drivers. That car placed BMW's larger (2.8 liter) six-cylinder engine in the E-21 3-series, providing extraordinary performance with total tractability. For serious BMW enthusiasts, that car represented a catharsis—a small BMW was at last equipped to compete against the cars from Porsche and come out ahead. With the 2.8-liter engine modified by Alpina to produce 200 horsepower, the B6 was endowed with staggering acceleration—Alpina quoted the distance from 0-100 kilometers per hour as taking only 7.2 seconds; independent road testers found the time to be closer to 6.9 seconds. With a top speed of "over 225 kilometers per hour," (and with a price ex-works of DM 48,750) the B6 was clearly positioned to compete directly against the most overtly sporting products from Europe's foremost manufacturers.

After September 1981, the B6 received a more highly-developed induction system, providing 218 horsepower (identical to the stock—and less highly tuned—BMW 3.5-liter engine).

Although once Alpina had engineered their big-block conversion, there was no mechanical problem associated with the installation of engines larger than 2.8-liters in the E-21 (external dimensions were essentially identical), the company did not formally offer any such package. Alpina's large-engine conversions on the E-21 set the model for years of subsequent development; the concept of BMW's largest engines in their smallest cars had always been successful (and had always found eager buyers).

The production figures for the B6 version of the E-21 3-series tell an interesting story—although very much more expensive, Alpina actually produced more of those cars than they produced of their C1 (using the smaller six-cylinder engines). Between November 1978 and January 1983, exactly 533 of Alpina's early B6s were built (including 324 units with the 200 horsepower engine and 209 with the later 218 horsepower motor).

Today, a well-preserved E-21 Alpina would be entirely suited either for daily driving or weekend enjoyment. The B6 versions would be the most desirable, with the only significant caveat concerning wet-weather handling. Given that even the U.S.-specification 320i was somewhat notorious for its ability to bring its rear end around under power in the wet, a 218bhp B6 would need to be treated with a great deal of respect under those circumstances. If, however, driving is to be kept primarily to dry conditions, a B6 would certainly provide enormous satisfaction.

THE DIETEL-ALPINA 345i

In conversations with Alpina, it becomes clear that the company has historically viewed the American market with a certain degree of detachment. While Alpina recognizes that there are many U.S. enthusiasts who would qualify as potential customers, the size of the U.S. market and the commitment necessary to service it has historically been greater than the company has wanted to take on. Despite Alpina's historic absence from the U.S. mar-

The Schnitzer-modified E21 323i Turbo.

ket, there have been U.S. BMW owners willing to work a bit harder (and pay a bit more) to obtain the company's products. Those products were probably most available between the mid-1970s and the mid-1980s (when the U.S. government closed down the business of privately importing cars).

Perhaps the best-known importer of Alpina cars and equipment into the U.S. was California-based Mike Dietel and his Dietel Enterprises operations. Any discussion of the large-engine E-21 3-series cars must include his considerable productive efforts. Throughout the 1980s, Dietel was considered one of the premier providers of tuned BMWs on the West Coast of the U.S. The special vehicles he built constituted his advertising program over a 15-year period.

Dietel was best known for his Alpina-equipped installations of BMW's large 6-cylinder engines in 3-series cars. These conversions were made using both factory stock and specially-tuned 2.8, 3.0, 3.3 and 3.5-liter engines, and were praised for their quality of construction. His cars used many Alpina components (and were generally referred to as Dietel-Alpinas), but Dietel did not restrict himself to that company's products if he felt something else was needed. During its heyday, Dietel Enterprises was a large-scale operation with over 20 mechanics, fully capable of engineering and fabricating whatever parts were needed for a special project. Dietel's cars were not just fitted with larger engines. In a conversation with me, he noted that he "did a total job, as far as going though the chassis, brakes and everything else."

Of special interest is the Dietel-Alpina 345i, a car created through the installation of BMW's most potent 2-valve engine (the turbocharged 3.5-liter 6-cylinder from the European 745i) into a U.S.-specification 320i. This car, the last project built by Dietel, received what can only be called a lavish array of equipment; the car's suspension, breaks and all ancillary components were comprehensively upgraded to full-race quality. The 345i's bodywork was enhanced through the use of custom-built box-type fender flares, allowing the fitting of enormous custom built BBS 3-piece wheels (15x9-inch front, 15x11-inch rear).

The combination proved compelling; contemporary road tests lauded the car for its performance and balance. The Dietel-Alpina 345i still exists today, and is believed to be privately owned in California.

THE FIRST-GENERATION 3-SERIES: OTHER EFFORTS

While Alpina's work with the E-21 3-series is best known, both Hartage and Schnitzer produced high-performance components and also prepared complete cars. It may be possible to locate a first-generation 3-series with such special equipment—a fully outfitted example (especially if the work was originally done by one of those companies) would be especially desirable. Although we are not aware of a separate catalogued model available from Hartage, Schnitzer did produce a number of 323i Turbo cars with the same specifications. Those cars (similar to the later E-30 version discussed below) utilized a KKK turbocharger and extensive modification to the rest of the engine. The complete package included a special Bilstein suspension, 15-inch tires on BBS alloy rims and a Zender spoiler kit.

THE SECOND-GENERATION 3-SERIES (E-30)

BMW introduced their new 3-series to the world in late 1982, with the production car appearing in the U.S. as a 1984 model. Following their enormous success with their E-21 3-series, it was unlikely that the company would stray too far afield from the original concept. In fact, BMW was initially criticized (particularly in the U.S.) for the conservatism of their approach. As with the updated 5-series (the E-28), some publications claimed not to be able to distinguish between the old and new cars.

However, as a new platform for those tuning efforts already applied to the original 3-series, the E-30 was a resounding success. The new car was more aerodynamic, better handling and (to some eyes) more attractively styled.

THE FIRST M3 (E-30)

The development of the original (E-30) M3 was heavily influenced by the factory's desire to successfully field a production-based car in motorsports. According to the BMW's press introduction; "the M3 is destined for touring car racing in more or less standard form, without too many modifications." As such, the M3 was fundamentally unlike any other factory 3-series. The cars were clearly built far more for competition and serious road use than for everyday transportation, and were configured appropriately. Where the standard E-30 3-series cars (325e, 325i, etc) were efficient, well-made standard small BMW sports sedans, the M3 was immediately recognizable as something else entirely. BMW's adverting said "Just one look tells you this is a very special car," and that was certainly the case. With its broad, squared-off fender flares (which dominated the car in profile), its large front and rear spoilers and lowered ride height, the M3 was a shamelessly aggressive-looking car. That impression was reinforced by almost everything about the car. Where the company's more luxurious 3-series cars were powered by smooth running six cylinder engines, the M3's engine was a derivation of their famous four-cylinder motor which had a well-proven competition record. That engine—using essentially the same block as the original 1960s 1500—took the form of a highly-tuned 2.3-liter 16-valve unit. The design featured a forged crankshaft running in five bearings, a special cast light-alloy oil sump (with baffle plates), and a 4-valve per cylinder head closely related to that fitted to the M1 engine. According to the company; "it goes without saying that experience gained in Formulas 1 and 2, where BMW's racing engines are also based on this original design, has gone into the development of the M3 power unit."

With 200bhp (non-catalyst version) available to motivate a car weighing about 2,700 pounds, the performance capabilities of the original M3 justified the use of those specialized components. The car was able to accelerate from 0-100 kilometers per hour in only 6.7 seconds, and could produce a top speed of 146 miles per hour. Introduced in Germany in December 1996, production lasted until December 1990.

At the end of its production run, BMW built a limited number of M3 Evolution models. Those cars, built to homologate various components for Group A racing, included 505 examples of the M3 Evolution (produced from February to May 1987 and provided with 200bhp engines), 501 examples of the M3 Evolution II (produced from March to May 1988 with 220bhp, an additional lower rear spoiler and lightweight body panels), and 600 of the ultimate version, the M3 Sport Evolution. Those 600 cars—produced from January to March 1990, each of which was individually numbered with a special plaque on the interior console—were equipped with larger engines (2.5-liters vs. 2.3-liters) producing greater horsepower (238bhp). Sport Evolution M3s were also provided with an

Herbert Schnitzer with Hans-Joachim Stuck - inspecting the Schnitzer 323i Turbo.

The Schnitzer 323i Turbo engine, as installed in both the E-21 and E-30 323is.

The original M3—the most sporting production BMW since the 3.0CSL. Originally conceived for motorsport, and optimized for performance, the M3 provided BMW enthusiasts with cause for celebration. The 4-cylinder engine provided up to 200bhp.

unusual and very effective Electronic Damping Control suspension system. That system allowed the car's driver to select between three levels of suspension firmness from the cockpit. More aggressive bodywork (with larger spoilers and fender flares) and a revised interior completed the Sport Evolution III package.

When introduced, the M3 generated enormous excitement among BMW enthusiasts. Closer to a pure race car than anything ever offered by the factory (except perhaps the 3.0 CSL coupe), the M3 left an indelible mark on its intended audience. As of this writing, E-30 M3s are not especially sought after, and are widely available in both Europe and

The BMW 4-cylinder engine lineup. From left to right; the street, Formula 2 and Formula 1 versions—all based upon the same basic design and engine block.

The M3 interior and engine compartment. Almost everything about the car was designed to improve performance; very little was included in the way of extra convenience equipment which would add weight.

Various view of the original M3, seen here outfitted to European-specification.

the U.S. It seems likely that, over time, original M3s will come to be better appreciated both for their historical significance, and also for their exceptional dynamic qualities.

OTHER FACTORY EFFORTS ON THE E-30 PLATFORM

THE SOUTH AFRICAN 333i

BMW South Africa has long represented both a significant source of business for its parent company, and also a source of some of BMW's more interesting products. Built between 1985 and 1987, The BMW 333i represented a joint effort by BMW S.A., BMW Motorsport and Alpina. Essentially an E-30 3-series fitted with the large block 3.3-liter 6-cylinder engine (as standard in the 533i, 633CSi and 733i), the 333i built on the comparable earlier work done by Alpina.

Right
With its broad, squared-off fender flares (which dominated the car in profile), its large front and rear spoilers and lowered ride height, the M3 was a shamelessly aggressive-looking car.

The M3 was fundamentally unlike any other factory 3-series. The cars were clearly built far more for competition and serious road use than for everyday transportation.

The original E-30 M3, seen here in two of that model's most popular colors (see previous spread). The M3 was widely considered the most sporting production BMW since the 3.0CSL Batmobile.

The South African 333i should be viewed principally as a derivation of Alpina's similar car (the E-30 B6), and a great many Alpina components were incorporated. The 333i was unusual, in that it represented a far more overt utilization of Alpina's efforts than had been customary. While BMW essentially produced an Alpina design for the South African market with the 333i, it seems unlikely that they would have been willing to do the same on a wider scale. Indeed, the opportunity to expand production and distribution of the 333i was readily available; none of the components required for the car were especially difficult to produce or expensive (in the context of the price the 333i would have realized in the market), and favorable reviews had worked their way into the European automotive press (especially in the U.K.). At the conclusion of 333i production in

Smaller and lighter than subsequent models, and with up to 200bhp from its 16-valve 4-cylinder Motorsport engine, the first generation M3 is among the quickest of all recent BMWs on a winding road.

The E-30 M3 Sport Evolution III. Only 600 of these cars were built by BMW, each with larger 2.5-liter engines producing 238bhp. This was the ultimate road-going factory M3.

The sport steering wheel of the M3 Sport Evolution is unique to this model.

Right
The M3 Sport Evolution Interior. More aggressively bolstered seats provide additional support during hard cornering.

1987, 204 vehicles had been built, with many having gone into production racing in South Africa.

From a collector's perspective, the two South African BMWs worth locating would be the 333i and the 24-valve 745i. While very few of these cars are likely to have left South Africa (a handful of 333is may exist in Europe—in addition to the one car officially brought into England, it is estimated that perhaps five cars were privately imported into the U.K.—and none are believed to have been imported into the U.S.), they would doubtless provide an owner with a great deal of satisfaction.

U.S.-SPECIFICATION E-30 CARS

As was usual at the time, the U.S. market was denied access to the most interesting factory performance derivations. As a partial measure, BMW did offer optional sport-packages on their U.S-specification E-30 cars. These were made available on the 325es, the 325is and the 318is (the latter being a separate model, rather than an option package on an existing model). The sport options included larger alloy wheels, more aggressively-contoured seating and sport suspension packages. No modifications were made in terms of engine outputs. While these cars are not nearly so desirable as the true factory specials, they offer interesting (and readily available) alternatives to comparable base model 3-series.

THE ITALIAN MARKET 320iS

One of the most interesting factory derivations on the E-30 platform remains the Italian market-only 320iS. This car (which bore no similarity to the E-21 U.S.-specification car of the same name), was created to take advantage of the very large tax reduction on cars with engine displacements under 2.0 liters. In this instance, BMW reduced the displacement of their hugely successful 2.5 liter M3 engine to 1,990cc by sleeving (decreasing) the bore.

For this unusual and frequently overlooked invention, BMW quoted performance figures of 7.9 seconds from 0-62 miles per hour and a top speed of 141 miles per hour. Slower, certainly, than an M3 from the same year, but quicker than the 325i which it most closely resembled.

The most compelling feature of the 320iS was almost certainly its bodywork; rather than the M3's conspicuously aggressive fender flares and spoiler package, the 320iS came equipped with only front and rear spoilers to differentiate it from its 3-series siblings. Both of those items could be deleted upon request.

With its smaller displacement M3 engine combined with box-stock 3-series bodywork, the 320iS represents an interesting hybrid. From an end-users perspective, the car must be considered more desirable than any factory production E-30 3-series, with the exceptions of the M3 and the South African 333i. It is doubtful that many 320iS currently exist outside of Italy (and few probably

The E-30 3-series-based Alpina C2 2.7. With 210bhp, the Alpina car was a significantly better performer than the standard version.

Only 160 of the E-30 3-Series-based Alpina C2 2.7 cars were built.

Alpina's E-30-based B6 2.8. A most subtle approach to performance than BMW's own M3. Without the fender flares, the Alpina B6 was nonetheless even more powerful (with 210bhp) and slightly faster than the Motorsport 3-series.

The Alpina B6 3.5. Based on BMW's second-generation 3-series, the B6 offered the company's largest engine in their smallest car. With 254bhp, the Alpina-tuned car offered exceptional performance.

there). None are believed to have been imported into the U.S.

THE SMALL-BLOCK E-30 ALPINA CARS

Alpina's C1 version of the original 323i had been among their most popular models, so it was reasonable to expect that their follow-up version would be well received. With the second-generation (E-30) 3-series, Alpina appears to have focused their efforts on the small-six model, rather than on any of the four-cylinder cars (no four-cylinder E-30 Alpinas are catalogued).

Between August 1993 and June 1992, Alpina produced several versions of small-six E-30-based cars. Those included their C1 2.3 (2316 cc, 170bhp, 35 built), C1 2.5 (2494 cc, 190bhp, 50 built), C2 2.5 (2552 cc, 185bhp, 74 built), C2 2.7 (2693 cc, 210bhp, 108 built), C2 2.7 with catalyst (2693 cc, 204bhp, 52 built), and their B3 2.7 with catalyst (2693 cc, 204bhp, 257 built). All of the above cars were essentially similar—being based on very nearly the same platform with different versions of the same basic engine. Looking at production figures, it is clear that as BMW and Alpina were able to increase the displacement of the small block six-cylinder engine, demand for tuned versions grew proportionately. Despite the obvious appeal of these cars, Alpina's more potent large-block 3-series conversions have garnered more attention (and are today more in demand).

THE E-30 ALPINA B6

BMW second-generation replacement for the original 3-series provided Alpina with an equally good platform for their excellent B6 conversion. As with the earlier car, Alpina provided a complete, well-engineered package, including improvements to the suspension (including Alpina progressive rate springs, specially-valved Bilstein shock absorbers, Alpina light-alloy wheels), brakes, interior, etc. As with the earlier car, the large-engine Alpina conversion yielded an agile and very fast car.

The second-generation B6 was produced in two series; the first with their specially-tuned version of the BMW 2.8-liter large-block 6-cylinder (producing 210bhp), and the second with their version of the BMW 3.5-liter engine (producing 254bhp). Between March 1984 and July 1986, Alpina built 259 examples of the 2.8-liter B6. The company built an additional 132 examples of their 3.5-liter B6 between November 1985 and July 1987 (not including the M3-based cars discussed below).

THE E-30 ALPINA M3s

For Alpina, the introduction of the M3 must have come as both a blessing and a curse. Here, on the one hand, was a factory-stock vehicle which had as much serious semi-race quality hardware as could be desired (leaving that much less for Alpina to do). On the other hand, there could have hardly

A Schnitzer-prepared E-30 convertible. The car is equipped with the Schnitzer cylinder head kit providing 190bhp.

An E-30 Touring with full Schnitzer modifications, including the company's S3 2.7-liter engine with 210bhp.

been a better platform for Alpina's big-block conversion. With the M3-based B6S, the company applied their well-proven two-valve, 3.5-liter conversion (yielding approximately 254bhp with moderate tuning work) to what many consider BMW's best road car. The resulting B6S stands as one of Alpina's finest efforts ever. Although previous B6 big-block 3-series conversions were generally very well-regarded, the B6S had an almost perfect balance derived from the more aggressive nature of the M3. Between November 1987 and December 1990, Alpina built just 62 examples of their M3-based B6.

THE SECOND-GENERATION
HARTAGE 3-SERIES CARS

Large-Block Cars

With the second-generation 3-series, Hartage moved a bit closer towards that role traditionally occupied by Alpina; that of an autonomous automobile *manufacturer*. While the company's primary business remained the production and sale of tuning components, they were now building a considerable number of completed cars.

Hartage's most compelling offering based on the E-30 3-series (and was undoubtedly their incredible H35.) As with Alpina's similar B6, Hartage fitted BMW's largest (3.5-liter) engine to their smallest car—with predictably satisfying results. Unlike Alpina, however, Hartage were willing to indulge the desires of those who wanted still more power in a 3-series chassis.

Models within the H35 range included the 3.5-liter engine at various levels of tune. While most of

Hartage's business has been and continues to be in providing high-performance components, each H35 could be had only as a complete car. The most basic version of the H35 included a Hartage-tuned 12-valve engine (with special Mahle pistons and work to the cylinder head). In that form, the engine produced 260bhp, providing 0-60 miles per hour acceleration of about 6.0 seconds, and a top speed of approximately 150 miles per hour. With additional (and extensive) work to the suspension, drivetrain, rear axle, brakes and wheels and tires, the complete 260bhp H35 listed for about (U.K. Pounds) 31,000 in 1988.

The most exclusive Hartage model during that period was also a 3-series based H35, but fitted with a specially tuned version of the 24-valve M6 engine and producing an incredible 330bhp. With that much power in such a small, light vehicle, that car provided shattering performance—Hartage listed a top speed in excess of 170 miles per hour. An equally remarkable price was demanded for that car; about (U.K. Pounds) 45,000 in 1988.

Any version of the H35 would provide an interesting alternative to a similar large-engine Alpina car (there would be no equivalent at all to the 330bhp model). Production figures for the H35 are unfortunately not available.

Small-Block Cars

Beginning with the E-30 3-series, Hartage offered an "H26 Complete Conversion," for their BMW 325i, 325iX, 325i Touring and 325i Cabrio. That package included a 190bhp rework of the 2.5-liter BMW engine (with a Hartage engine control system, special camshaft, Hartage cylinder head gasket and valve cover, and a complete low-restriction exhaust system). The conversion provided an upgraded sports suspension, including specially-valved Hartage/Bilstein struts and shock absorbers, and sports springs. Also supplied were aluminum front and rear strut braces, a rear stabilizer (anti-roll) bar, harder rubber suspension bushings, and a conversion to the differential to increase locking from 25 percent to 40 percent. The H26 benefited from a completely revised braking system, with special Hartage calipers, disks and pads. Cosmetically (or functionally at higher speeds), the company fitted an aerodynamic body kit consisting of front and rear spoilers, and side and rear body skirts. H25s were given Hartage's attractive light-alloy wheels, their 4-spoke leather steering wheel and their leather gear lever knob.

In addition to the complete Hartage conversion, customers were free to mix and match essentially any combination of the above.

THE SCHNITZER 323i TURBO

While Alpina and Hartage each offered a range of complete cars based on the E-30 3-series, AC Schnitzer appears to have produced only a single catalogued model based on that car (although numerous individual specials were doubtless built). The Schnitzer 323i Turbo was, as its name suggests, a turbocharged variation on the BMW 6-cylinder 3-series. The cars were extensively modified, with the engine accounting for most of the effort and expense. The Schnitzer engine was very much more than a small six with a bolt-on turbo; the company built the motor using special pistons, a reshaped cylinder head, special main

and conrod bearings, a special cylinder head gasket, a KKK turbo unit, a Schnitzer exhaust system, an intercooler, oilcooler, an additional fan and an oversized radiator. Those components, together with the specially-modified Bosch L-Jetronic fuel injection system, provided 218bhp with a 7,5:1 compression ratio.

Schnitzer upgraded the rest of the car as well: suspension modifications consisted of Bilstein shock absorbers, front and rear progressive rate springs, and Pirelli P7 tires on 15-inch BBS alloy wheels. The 323i Turbo came with a Zender spoiler kit, including front and rear spoilers and sideskirts. Schnitzer quoted an acceleration figure from 0-100 kilometers per hour of 6.9 seconds, and a top speed of 238 miles per hour. In 1986, the company listed a price for the car of DM25,193.

Although the E-30 Schnitzer 323i Turbo is probably so rare that the purchase of one will never be an option, the car would provide considerable enjoyment for an enthusiast of high-performance BMWs.

THE SCHNITZER S3 SPORT 2.5

With the success of BMW first-generation M3 (both in competition and among enthusiasts), AC Schnitzer devoted considerable resources to the development of that model. While Schnitzer's M3-based S3 Sport 2.5 was not a completely separate model—in that all of the car's special components could be ordered separately—it appears that Schnitzer prepared a significant number of vehi-

The Schnitzer S3 Sport 2.5—based on the original BMW M3.

With 245bhp, the S3 would accelerate from 0-100 kilometers per hour in 6.7 seconds, and could achieve a top speed of approximately 250 kilometers per hour.

The second generation M3 has gained enormous popularity worldwide. Although larger and heavier than its E-30-based predecessor, the later car represents for many a return to BMW's high-performance roots.

cles to the full S3 Sport 2.5 specification. Further-more, the relationship between Schnitzer and BMW Motorsport with regard to this model sug-gests that it deserves to be considered as a com-plete car. According to Schnitzer:

The designers of the BMW M3 were faced with the task of developing a series-produced car with all the characteristics of a genuine competi-tion vehicle. During the development process, the Schnitzer team was called upon to check the pos-sibilities of the M3 down to the last detail. At the order of BMW Motorsport GmbH, the Freilass-ing team constructed M3 works cars, arranged for their servicing and entered several of them in the World and European Touring Car champi-onship. For a racing car in its first year, the BMW/Schnitzer M3 proved extraordinarily suc-cessful. The M3 not only achieved first place in its class, but also proved to be a serious threat to much more powerful vehicles.

The experience which the Schnitzer team ac-quired with the M3 provided additional infor-mation as to how the that car's performance could be enhanced even further in serial produc-tion -without any sacrifices in terms of reliability or driving behavior.

AC Schnitzer developed and refined these ideas and converted them into practical solu-tions. The S3 Sport 2.5 is a design which exploits the potential of the M3's 4-cylinder 4-valve en-gine to the fullest - by increasing the capacity to 2431cc. In addition, the precision machining of the cylinder head of the intake and exhaust sys-tem (widening, smoothing and exact fitting of the connections) produces an even more effective gas exchange than in the standard model.

Weight-optimized pistons with floor cooling and a distinctive beaded edge make for optimal combustion, while some of the increased stroke is compensated for through the design of the special AC Schnitzer connecting rods. The centerpiece, the AC Schnitzer crankshaft with 83mm stroke, is machined from solid steel to ensure greater rigidity and durability. The higher torque of this engine means that the car can be driven at low revs and still provide powerful acceleration throughout its operating range.

The design of the S3 Sport 2.5 allows for driving at very high speed. Together with Bilstein, AC Schnitzer has designed a sport chassis with a 20mm lower ride height. This advanced suspension system (engineering to provide neutral to very slight understeering behavior) enables the strong performance of the S3 Sport 2.5 to be utilized safely and comfortably on the road.

AC Schnitzer's S3 Sport 2.5 predated BMW's own 2.5-liter M3, and provided performance comparable to the Motorsport Division's best efforts. With 245bhp, the Schnitzer car would accelerate from 0-100 kilometer per hour in 6.7 seconds, and could achieve a top speed of approximately 250 kilometers per hour. If one could be located, it would certainly represent an interesting alternative to one of the M3 Evolution models.

THE THIRD-GENERATION (E-36) 3-SERIES

Introduced in 1992, BMW's third-generation 3-series represented a significant advance over the E-30 cars. Much more up-to-date aesthetically, the newer cars featured aerodynamic styling combined with a very efficient utilization of interior spaces. Whereas the second generation 3-series cars were essentially updated versions of the earlier models, the third generation 3-series represented an entirely new—and very well-received—range.

THE E-36 M3: EUROPEAN AND U.S. VERSIONS

In many ways, the new M3 represented a significant return to the principals upon which BMW's postwar business had been built. While the company's entire line had grown larger, heavier and ultimately less sporting, the third-generation M3 appears to have benefited from a redefinition of its place in the market. At almost 3200 pounds, the car is not really comparable with the 2002tii, the 2002 Turbo or even the original (E-30) M3. Even so, the E-36 M3 has been proclaimed the legitimate beneficiary of the reputation created by those cars. In fact, and notwithstanding assertions by the automotive press, the E-36 M3 is in no way the successor to earlier, smaller and more visceral BMWs. It is, however, a remarkably good car, and one which deserves to be judged by a different set of standards—as the logical progression of the company's line of high-performance coupes. As a continuation of a product line began in the 1930s and maintained through the 2000CS, the 3.0CSi/CSL and the M6, the M3 existence makes far more sense.

After some concern that the second-generation M3 would never be brought into the U.S., the U.S.-specification M3 turned out to be an extreme-

Probably the most desirable of all recent BMWs, the limited-production M3 lightweight.

The M3L would reach 0-60 miles per hour in 5.8 seconds (against 6.1 for the standard M3), and a top speed of over 145 miles per hour, compared to the quoted 137 miles per hour for the standard car.

ly capable car. The primary difference between the RoW and U.S. M3s lay in their cylinder heads; the U.S. car utilized a less exotic (and very much less expensive) head, and developed 240bhp compared with 286bhp for the European version. The U.S. car, however, has the more flexible torque characteristics (along with different gearing) with the result that it is at least as fast in acceleration up to about 100 miles per hour.

THE E-36 M3: DRIVING IMPRESSIONS
(U.S.-Specification)

By early 1995, the new M3 had been universally lauded; almost every automotive publication

Alpina's third-generation 3-series, here seen is B6 2.8 form. Now with 240bhp, Alpina continues to develop superb cars based on BMW's basic platforms.

The Alpina B3 3.0 sedan. With 250bhp from Alpina's 3-liter 6-cylinder engine, the B3 was capable of accelerating from 0-100 kilometers per hour in 6.1 seconds. A top speed of over 255 kilometers per hour (160 miles per hour) was listed. *Alpina Automobile Meisterwerke catalog*

had heaped praise upon the car, with many naming it their "car of the year." M3 sales surged, both in Europe and in the U.S.

Even in U.S.-specification form, the M3 is very much a high-rpm car. In fact, the car actually feels (incorrectly) less robust in the lower portion of its range than its 325i sibling. That said, performance from the six-cylinder engine is virtually faultless, with very strong acceleration available in almost any situation. The upper portion of the car's rev range is especially robust, with the ability to pass almost anything on the road once the tachometer has passed 3,000rpm. It should be noted that performance is accompanied by a degree of mechanical smoothness which clearly surpasses the M3's Motorsports predecessors.

If the M3 disappoints in any way, it is not in its performance or handling. Nor can any fault be found in its workmanship; the quality of the M3

333bhp in a 4-door 3-series. Alpina's ultimate 3-series is currently the B8 4.6.

Alpina's B3 3.0, seen here in Cabriolet form. Modifications from the standard 3-series specification are as per the B3 3.0 sedan. *Alpina Automobile Meisterwerke catalog*

The car combines Alpina's version of the BMW V-8 engine (with increased displacement and special tuning) with the 3-series sedan.

Right
AC Schnitzer's S3 Sport CLS provided spectacular performance, reaching 0-100 kilometers per hour in 5.8 seconds and a top speed of 272 kilometers per hour.

The Schnitzer S3 Sport CLS—side view. Visible here are the wide Kevlar fender flares which allow Schnitzer to fit 9X18-inch rims at the front and 10X18-inch wheels at the rear.

The Schnitzer S3 Sport CLS interior door panel. The extent of Schnitzer's modifications are visible here; the entire panel is constructed of very light weight carbon fiber.

A view from the rear of the Schnitzer S3 Sport CLS. Modifications from the standard E-36 M3 include the company's Kevlar rear skirt with integrated rear bumper, Kevlar rear spoiler and roof spoiler and Schnitzer's quick filler fuel cap.

The Schnitzer S3 Sport CLS viewed from above.

A view of the Schnitzer S3 Sport CLS interior.

is fully up to the standards of modern BMWs. There can be no doubt that M3 owners are thrilled by the car, and that it will live up to almost anyone's expectations. For all its abilities, however, the M3 is very much a production car. That may seem a strange criticism for a car intended to be produced in the many thousands (and the workmanship is superb), but the M3 undeniably lacks the distinctive character of its predecessors. The original M5 and M6 seemed more specialized, more obviously hand-built. The conspicuous care given by Motorsport (and by Alpina) to details which would probably never even be seen set their cars apart from their production-based versions.

Various views of the Schnitzer S3 Sport CLS II.

The most visible changes from the original CLS include the larger front and rear spoilers and the very different color scheme.

Visible here is the Kevlar center console with Schnitzer's special switch panel, the Kevlar radio cover, the suede covered sports steering wheels, the aluminum pedal assembly and the specially-modified analog/digital dashboard display.

Where the first CLS was available only in a special shade of light grey, the second version was painted an unusual high-gloss flat green.

The CLS II was similar to the CLS, but offered even more power and greater weight reduction.

THE M3L

At the time of this writing, BMW had recently introduced what is likely the most interesting and desirable version of the E-36 3-series to date; the M3 Lightweight (M3L). The car has been specially built by BMW M "for the serious racer or driving school participant." The car is essentially similar to the standard M3, but is built without some of that car's equipment, including the sunroof, air conditioning, some insulation and the radio. The M3L includes aluminum, rather than the regular M3's steel doors.

The result of those changes is a weight reduction of approximately 225 pounds—from 3,175 pounds to 2,950 pounds. Additionally, the M3 Lightweight benefits from a lower (numerically higher) final drive ratio of 3.23, compared with

3.15 for the regular production M3. While the standard M3 and the M3L share the same 240bhp engine, BMW lists that figure with an asterisk in their sales literature with regard to the M3L. The company states that for that car "engines are selected at the upper end of design tolerance." In other words, BMW hand-picks the most powerful engines off the production line and designates them for the M3L.

Performance figures for the M3L should be somewhat better than for the standard M3. The factory lists 0-60 miles per hour acceleration of 5.8 seconds (against 6.1 for the standard car), and a top speed of "over 145 miles per hour" (as against a quoted 137 miles per hour for the standard car).

While final production figures for the M3L

had not been established at the time of this writing, it is believed that a total of 85 examples were to have been imported into the U.S.

THE THIRD-GENERATION ALPINA 3-SERIES

Based on the BMW E-36 3-series, Alpina's B3 3.0 provided that already very competent small sedan with even higher capabilities. As with Alpina's previous efforts, the B3 3.0 (which was preceded by an essentially identical B3 2.8 with 200cc less displacement) significantly expanded on both performance and handling. In this case, Alpina equipment included a 2997cc, 4-valve 6-cylinder motor, with a compression ratio of 10.5:1. With the benefit of Alpina's comprehensive modifications, that engine produced 250bhp at 5700rpm, and enabled the B3 3.0 to accelerate from 0-100 kilometers per hour in only 6.1 seconds. Alpina listed a top speed of over 255 kilometers per hour (160 miles per hour). As usual, all relevant subsystems of the car were completely modified, with significant changes made to the suspension system (Bilstein gas pressure shocks), brakes, transmission and wheels and tires.

The B3 3.0 was also available in convertible form, with specifications identical to the sedan version.

THE SCHNITZER S3 SPORT CLS AND CLS II

While Schnitzer has and continues to offer a number of models based on a set program of modifications, the company's special components are also available separately—enabling partial modification and confusing the issue of what constitutes a Schnitzer car. The company's most recent catalog, however, lists a single model which is "available as a complete car only, and exclusively ex-Aachen"—the S3 Sport CSL. Originally presented at the 1993 Frankfurt Auto Show, that car represents the most desirable of Schnitzer's recent efforts. Based on BMW's E-36 M3, the S3 Sport CLS involves a complete rework to a very high standard, and adds considerably to the capabilities of that car.

According to Schnitzer:

The AC Schnitzer S3 Sport CSL combines thoroughbred performance in truly sporting style with no sacrifice of suitability for everyday use. The central engineering concept behind the development of the S3 Sport CLS involves the dramatic improvement of the car's power to weight ra-

tio. In practice, this means that the vehicle must be light, but must also have ample reserves of power. The weight is reduced through the use of special aircraft-quality materials, such as carbon fiber and aluminum, making the S3 Sport CLS 128 kg lighter than the standard car.

The S3 Sport CLS developments are all based on the BMW M3. Extensive modifications and developments to the engine, suspension, interior and body styling make the S3 Sport CLS a unique vehicle.

Sport camshafts, a special exhaust system with a unique manifold and modified engine electronics bring about a dramatic improvement in engine performance, and provide thrilling performance. The modified power unit now puts out 236Kw/320bhp, rather than the standard 210Kw/286bhp. Our motorsport-derived gearshift lever shortens the gear lever travel, and thus the time spent changing from one gear to another.

In every important aspect, the S3 Sport CLS reflects the motorsport experience and philosophy of AC Schnitzer. With every detail, we have attempted to bridge the gap between the performance road car and the competition car.

AC Schnitzer's S3 Sport CLS lived up to the company's promises. Not only did the car provide spectacular performance (0-100 kilometers per hour in 5.8 seconds and a top speed of 272 kilometers per hour), it was a remarkably complete automobile. The amount of work which the company obviously lavished on the car's engine, brakes, suspension, interior and bodywork is extraordinary.

With the same displacement (2990cc), the CLS II provided 30 additional horsepower (now at 350bhp).

Schnitzer built a total of only 14 S3 Sport CLSs (all finished in the same light grey color), all of which were sold in Europe and Asia.

Following the success of the CLS, AC Schnitzer announced a Mark 2 version of the CLS. The CLS II was similar to the original car, but offered even more power and greater weight reduction. With the same displacement (2990cc), the CLS II provided 30 additional horsepower (now at 350bhp). Curb weight now stood at 135 kilograms less than the standard M3 on which the car was based. The CLS II was again offered only as a complete car, and now only in an unusual (but striking) shade of flat green. As of early 1996, Schnitzer listed a price for the CLS II of DM 225,000.

Curb weight now stood at 135 kilograms less than the standard M3 on which the car was based.

The Schnitzer S3 Sport CLS II interior.

The exterior color scheme is seen carried into the interior of the car.

The Schnitzer S3 Sport CLS II was fitted with an electronically adjustable rear wing. The adjustable wing is seen here in both positions.

Below
At 50 miles per hour the rear truck spoiler deploys to increase downforce.

CHAPTER 8

The 6-Series Coupes

For BMW, replacing their line of highly success-ful E-9 coupes represented a major undertak-ing. While there was probably never much ques-tion about mechanical configuration (the new coupes would be based on the E-12 5-series plat-form, and would use well-proven components), the visual design of the car was of vital importance. For a company such as BMW, relying on a relative-ly few number of models which are expected to re-main in production for far longer than those from American or Japanese manufacturers, the success of each new model takes on a far greater signifi-cance. Moreover, while the 6-series (as with its pre-decessor) was expected to sell in the smallest quan-tities of any of BMW's models, its position at the top of their product line endowed the car with a special significance in the market. The presence of the sleek 6-series coupe in BMW dealers' show-rooms probably helped to sell a great many much less expensive 3- and 5-series cars.

From the start, the new 6-series was intended to be a larger and heavier car than its predecessor. With the impending possibility of increasingly

A well-kept European-specification M6. Note the 415mm 3-piece alloy wheels. U.S.-market cars were fitted with one-piece alloys in the same size.

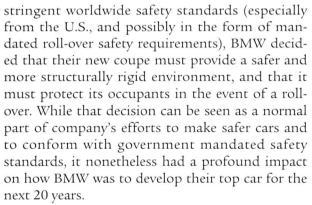

The 635CSi, seen from several angles. This car, continually developed and refined, provided BMW with a flagship coupe for many years.

The 635CSi was part of the 6-series which formed the basis for some of the most interesting cars from BMW's Motorsport Division and Alpina.

stringent worldwide safety standards (especially from the U.S., and possibly in the form of mandated roll-over safety requirements), BMW decided that their new coupe must provide a safer and more structurally rigid environment, and that it must protect its occupants in the event of a roll-over. While that decision can be seen as a normal part of company's efforts to make safer cars and to conform with government mandated safety standards, it nonetheless had a profound impact on how BMW was to develop their top car for the next 20 years.

Upon its introduction, the 6-series did not meet with overwhelming acclaim. Where the earlier coupe could just about straddle the line between grand tourer and sports car (with the lightweight 3.0CSL blurring the line still further), the 6-series was (and would only ever be) a grand tourer. Subsequent iterations of the car would be more powerful, better handling and more aggressive, but the basic and inviolate dimensions of the new car fixed its role in the automotive continuum.

If finding a road-car replacement of BMW's successful E-24 6-cylinder coupe was difficult, than finding an appropriate race track substitute was almost impossible. The new 6-series, for all of its appeal as a road car, was not at all suited for serious competition. This fact was not lost on those racing 3.0-liter coupes; they continued to develop that platform long after the introduction of its replacement.

THE 6-SERIES CARS: FACTORY EFFORTS

Throughout the life of the 6-series, BMW and the Motorsport Division made available a variety of performance options. These principally included larger alloy wheels and tires, sport suspension packages and various accessories such as Motorsport steering wheels. At the same time, the Motorsport Division created a very small number of specially prepared 6-series cars for special customers (those could include BMW executives and factory race drivers). We would be careful to distinguish 6-series cars which had received certain performance options from those vehicles which had been specially prepared at the Motorsport facility. While cars fitted with Motorsport options are indeed desirable, legitimate (and preferably documented) complete special Motorsport cars are much more highly coveted.

THE M635CSi and M6

While BMW's 635CSi had been regarded as among the best sports coupes since its introduction in 1979, the 6-series had come under increasing competitive pressure by the mid-1980s. Porsche's 928 had been continually updated by that company, so that by 1984 the 928 was both very much faster and better handling than the 635CSi. BMW could not help but be acutely aware of the comparison, as it was made in almost every magazine article featuring the 6-series. The company's solution was both straightforward and consistent with their historical approach to higher performance; upgrade an existing platform with proven components.

Introduced in 1984, the M635CSi (later changed to M6) stood at the top of BMW's product range. The company announced that "the flagship of the "M" line is BMW Motorsport's special version of the BMW 6-series coupe. This ultimate BMW luxury performance coupe is outwardly similar to the familiar 6-series coupe (the 635CSi) except for certain significant details, such as its wide, large-diameter cross-spoke forged alloy wheels, correspondingly low and wide tires, a discreet spoiler on its rear deck and its M6 emblem".

The reason for the company's enthusiasm lay under the car's hood; BMW Motorsport had combined the 6-series body and chassis with their race-proved 24-valve six-cylinder engine (designated S38). Derived from the M1's powerplant (and before that, from the racing 3.0CSLs), the M635CSi's engine was now controlled by Bosch Motronic fuel-injection. While displacement was unchanged at 3453cc, the M635CSi engine benefited from its updated injection system; "The 9 bhp power increase as compared to the M1 road version (now 286bhp at 6500rpm) was achieved through the new design of the entire induction and exhaust systems together with the use of digital engine electronics. The engine's power-to-displacement ratio is 61kW/liter, and its torque-to-displacement ratio is 98Nm/liter. The M635CSi accelerates from 0 to 100 kilometers per hour in 6.4 seconds, and has a top speed of 158 miles per hour."

It should be noted that, although the M635CSi and M6 were made in relatively large numbers compared with previous Motorsport specials, the engine was indeed an exceptional piece of engineering. That engine differed significantly from its regular production 3.5-liter sibling, featuring:
· A short-stroke design: the S38 has a shorter stroke and larger bore than the BMW 3.5-liter

The M635CSi; BMW's ultimate 6-series coupe. The combination of the company's competition-based, 24-valve 3.5-liter engine (producing 286bhp) with the coupe chassis proved very attractive.

Capable of accelerating from 0-60 miles per hour in only 6.1 seconds, and with a top speed of 158 miles per hour, there were very few vehicles which could rival these Motorsport cars.

Developed directly from BMW's competition effort. The 4-valve Motorsport engine, as fitted to both the M5 and M6.

The U.S.-market M6, which did not become available until after the car had been on sale in Europe for several years. The European M6 was among the most widely-imported of all grey market BMWs, and U.S. enthusiasts were grateful when BWM decided to bring that model in themselves.

single-overhead-cam engine, and slightly larger displacement.

· Dual overhead camshafts, chain-driven
· Four valves per cylinder in V-formation, actuated by cup-type lifters
· Hemispherical combustion chambers
· High compression ratio (10.5:1 for the European market, 9.8:1 for the U.S.)
· An individual throttle plate for each cylinder
· Machined intake and exhaust ports
· Honed cylinders
· Dual exhaust system
· Low-restriction catalytic converter
· Oil cooler in front spoiler.

While the most prominent feature of the M635CSi/M6 was clearly its race-bred engine, BMW's Motorsport Division paid equal attention to upgrading the car's chassis. That chassis, while similar in layout to other 6-series cars (and also to the 5-series), received substantial detail work so as to cope with very much higher power levels.

According to the division:

In its fundamentals, the M6 chassis is like that of all larger BMW models, with double-pivot strut-type front suspension and Track Link semi-trailing arm independent rear suspension linked to a rigid unitized steel body-chassis. Compared with the 635CSi, the M6 sits 0.4 inches lower, and its rear springs are progressive-rate for firmer handling without sacrificing riding comfort over small bumps. Bilstein gas-pressure

shock absorbers are fitted all around; the front ones are the twin-tube type, whose two sets of valving allow separate calibration of shock action over small and large bumps - again, a feature that achieves an optimum combination of handling and ride.

For exceptional straight-line stability at very high speeds, Motorsport engineered in extra steering caster and gave the variable-assist steering even firmer road feel. The front ventilated disc brakes have been enlarged from 11.2 in. to 11.8 inches in diameter, and the standard anti-lock braking system is specially calibrated for the M6 suspension, tires and brakes. Completing the running gear are extra-wide cross-spoke forged alloy wheels, size 415 X 210 TR, with Michelin TRX 240/45VR-415 tires.

The M635CSi/M6 cars are today highly sought after by BMW enthusiasts. Among the most popular (and available) of all Motorsport models, they continue to represent a compelling option for those seeking very high performance in a BMW coupe.

THE ALPINA 6-SERIES CARS:

Following Alpina's success with BMW's original 6-cylinder E-9 coupe, their involvement with the company's new 6-series was inevitable. Just as the 633CSi was BMW's showpiece, so too would it form the basis for Alpina's ultimate effort thus far.

Some of Alpina's most interesting work was displayed to its best advantage on BMW's second generation coupe; except for the motorsport cars, the 6-series was never as aggressively outfitted as some would have liked. From very soon after the car's introduction in 1976 (and especially with the availability of Alpina's turbocharged variants from 1978 to 1988), Alpina provided all that anyone could have wanted in a BMW coupe.

While the company's first efforts on the new coupe involved special (non-cataloged) work at the request of individual clients (as with the earlier 5-series sedan), Alpina was quick to offer a complete package for the new 6-series. By May of 1977, the company was already listing a "BMW 630/Alpina." That car (also referred to as the 630 CS B2), came equipped with Alpina's Type B2 motor. The B2 retained the standard displacement of 2,986 cc, but was fitted with special Solex carburetors on an Alpina induction system, a compression ratio of 9.5:1, an Alpina camshaft and the usual porting and

polishing work to the head. In that state of tune, the B2 provided 230bhp, and endowed the Alpina 630 with a top speed of 230 kilometers per hour and acceleration from 0 to 100 kilometers per hour of 6.9 seconds (both figures with a 3.45:1 rear end ratio). The car was additionally equipped with virtually every item from Alpina's extensive catalog; 7x14-inch alloy wheels, an Alpina front spoiler, a full interior upgrade package and a special Bilstein-Alpina suspension systems were all included.

In essentially all respects, Alpina's first complete car based upon BMW's 6-series was very similar to their later efforts. Looking at the 1977 and the 1985 versions side-by-side, the only visible difference would have been that the earlier car lacked the Alpina rear spoiler (developed later), and that later cars were equipped with larger wheels of (15-inch and 16-inch diameters). The primary mechanical difference between the early Alpina 630 CS B2

An early (circa 1977) Alpina-prepared 6-series, the 230bhp 630 CS B2. Similar to Alpina's work on the early 5-series sedan, the coupe was also equipped with a specially-tuned fuel-injected 3-liter engine, and was capable of 0-100 kilometers per hour acceleration in 6.9 seconds.

and the later B9 coupe lay with their engines; while the B2 relied on 3.0 liters and carburetion, the B9 used the later 3.5-liter fuel injected motor. With the earlier car providing 230bhp and the later version offering 245bhp, they were in fact very close in every category.

While production figures for the 630 CS B2 are unavailable (although listed as a complete package in Alpina's literature for that period, the car does not appear as a cataloged model), it seems likely that no more than perhaps a hundred such cars were constructed. The identification of such a car today is made easier by the fact that Alpina were (by then) fitting separate serial number plaques to the dashboards of their cars. As always, the best indicator of authenticity remains the original paperwork that would have accompanied any Alpina-prepared car.

ALPINA'S B7 AND B7S
TURBOCHARGED 6-SERIES CARS

While Alpina components undoubtedly found their way onto the 6-series almost from the moment of that car's introduction, the first full Alpina conversion of the new coupe (bearing its own identification number) was made available in December 1978. That car, labeled the B7 Turbo, went considerably further towards resurrecting the spirit of the 3.0CSL than did BMW's own 635CSi. In terms of 6-series performance cars, Alpina's B7 remained the unchallenged leader until BMW's in-

troduction of the M635CSi/M6 (a car entirely different in character from the B7, though not necessarily any faster).

The 6-series B7 Turbo represented a complete transformation of the 633CSi. In building the car, Alpina changed both virtually every major mechanical component, and also the fundamental character of the car. As with the B7 version of the 5-series (for which the same engine was used), Alpina initially utilized the 3.0-liter version of the BMW inline 6-cylinder engine. Alpina replaced the Bosch electronic fuel injection system used by BMW with a Pierburg mechanical system better suited to the precise requirements of the installed turbocharged. The entire engine was carefully rebuilt using components specifically designed for the engine, including lower-compression Mahle pistons. Alpina gave their customers a considerable degree of discretion when it came to operating their cars; every B7 came fitted with an adjustable boost system which regulated the turbocharger from between 0.45 bars to 0.90 bars of boost (corresponding to between 220-300bhp for the B7, and between 250-330bhp for the B7S).

B7s were available with either the close-ratio or the overdrive 5-speed manual gearbox. It is not believed that any cars were fitted with automatic transmissions.

As would be expected, the 6-series-based B7 provided extraordinary performance. The Alpina coupe was capable of sprinting from 0-100 kilometers per hour in only 6.2 seconds, and could produce a top speed of 265 kilometers per hour.

While the B7 was certainly more sporting and more aggressive package than the 633CSi or 635CSi, it was also very different from BMW's own M6. Those differences were largely a function of engines; as a turbocharged derivation of the production 2-valve engine, the B7 motor was less sporting (or less frantic, depending on your perspective) than the 4-valve Motorsport product from BMW. Both are viciously fast and entirely usable as regular transportation, although the M6 would probably be the choice for someone who planned to use their car on an everyday basis; the B7 is probably too rare for that sort of exposure. Either would provide their owners with a full measure of the qualities which have built BMW's postwar performance reputation.

In terms of exclusivity, the Alpina B7 wins

A carbureted Alpina large 6-cylinder engine. This is the 230bhp B2 motor fitted to early 5- and 6-series Alpinas.

hands down. *Over a ten-year period,* a total of only 313 cars were built. For the enthusiast considering ownership today, a B7 would likely provide not only considerable pride of ownership, but also a great deal of satisfaction as a usable vehicle with remarkable capabilities.

THE ALPINA 6-SERIES CARS:
B9 AND B10 NATURALLY ASPIRATED

Alpina's turbocharged 6-series not only predated the company's naturally aspirated version of the car, it also outsold it by a considerable margin. With a total of only 119 B9s and B10s built between 1982 and 1987, Alpina was clearly not overwhelmed by demand for the cars. These figures become more interesting when compared with Alpina's output of non-turbocharged E-28-based 5-series sedans over the same period—a total of 577 cars.

The reason for buyers' preference for the more expensive car can likely be found by looking at what it is they were buying. Alpina customers have historically expected the company's products to provide them with the definitive version of a particular BMW. It may therefore be understandable that those who sought out Alpina's version of BMW's performance coupe would not request anything but their top-of-the-line. Towards the end of their production, demand for the 635i-based B9 and B10s were likely also effected by BMW's own M635i.

In any case, either the B9 or the B10—with 245 and 261bhp, respectively—would have been able to keep up with almost anything on the road (except for a B7).

THE 6-SERIES CARS; OTHER EFFORTS

One of the most logical engine transplants for the 6-series would have been to provide that car with the turbocharged 3.5-liter engine from the 745i. While this combination was almost certainly tried by BMW themselves, the idea was never pursued either by the factory or by the tuners. The installation would not have been very difficult, how-

Alpina's 6-series-based B7 Turbo. With even more power than BMW's M635CSi (up to 330bhp), the Alpina version challenged the most exotic sports cars in terms of performance. Heavily modified in almost all respects by Alpina, total production was limited to only 313 cars over a ten year period.

ever, and at least a few tuners and individuals did create their own "645CSis." With the turbocharged engine providing 252bhp in stock form, a 6-series so modified would have been about as quick as a factory U.S.-specification M6, and not too far behind a European-specification M635CSi or M6. Moreover, the nature of the 2-valve turbocharged engine was significantly different from the 4-valve Motorsport engine; being a bit less linear in power delivery (a function of forced induction), but also a more relaxed, less busy powerplant. Compared with the M6, the installation of the turbocharged engine in the 6-series would have made for a somewhat less responsive, less sporting car. At the same time, the 645CSi would have had a less urgent character than the 4-valve M6, and would doubtless have made a very fine and fast grand tourer.

CHAPTER 9

The High-Performance 7-Series Cars

THE FIRST 7-SERIES

After a production run of eight years, BMW's new E-23 7-series replaced the company's successful and popular E-3 line of large sedans in 1976. While European drivers could chose from a wide range of configurations (engine sizes from 2.8- to 3.5-liters and equipment levels ranging from spartan to lavish), the U.S. market was sent only the fully equipped 733i (and later the 735i). In almost any configuration, the 7-series immediately distinguished itself as an exceptional effort. Contemporary road testers lauded the car's performance, its handling, and the availability of a 4-or 5-speed manual transmission (very unusual in a large luxury car). The U.S. automotive press was especially enthusiastic, rating the car above the contemporary Mercedes 450SEL and the Jaguar XJ6 models. In fact, the original 7-series may have been the first modern sports/luxury car built—establishing a category which has grown mightily over the past 20 years.

While the standard-model 7-series were all strong performers, some demand clearly existed for an even faster and more capable large BMW sedan. The results of that demand follow.

The Alpina B12 5.0—the company's ultimate 7-series. Special tuning of the 5.0-liter 12-cylinder engine produces 350bhp, and enables the car to accelerate from 0-100 kilometers per hour in 6.9 seconds.

BMW's first-generation (E-23) 7-series, seen here demonstrating its cornering ability. This car is identified as an early car by its narrow kidney-shaped grill. The 745i was externally virtually identical to the other 7-series models.

A MORE AMBITIOUS 7-SERIES

By the late 1970s, the 7-Series had firmly established its position near the top of the luxury sedan segment. Together with the S-Class Mercedes (usually the 450 SEL) and the Jaguar XJ6, the car was considered among the best available.

Within this segment, however, competition has been and remains intense; manufacturers continuously develop and refine their products to satisfy the requirements of a demanding customer base. In contemporary road tests, the 735i (then the top-of-the-line 7-Series) distinguished itself on the basis of its agility and sporting response. Unlike its two primary competitors, the car was available with a manual transmission (overdrive 5-speed).

By the mid-1970s, both Mercedes and Jaguar (the two companies which have historically been most closely identified as competitors to BMW)

An early 7-series in profile. Later cars gained larger alloy wheels.

had larger-engine versions of their range-leading sedans. The Jaguar XJ12 used that company's enormously smooth and refined 5.3-liter V-12 engine, while the Mercedes 450 SEL 6.9 gained a huge (6.9-liter) V-8 engine generating massive torque and providing effortless acceleration.

Almost certainly in response to both these cars, BMW began development of a 12-cylinder engine of their own. This engine was the subject of a massive development campaign aimed at producing the first German 12-cylinder automobile since before World War II. With the company's well-proven 6-cylinder engine reaching the maximum of its development potential (given the limitations of existing technology and the use of a two valve-per-cylinder layout), BMW's decision to build a 12-cylinder power plant was clearly based on more then just marketing considerations. Prototype engines showed enormous promise, and were experimentally fitted to a range of different vehicles (mostly 7-series, but possibly also 5- and 6-series cars).

Installed for development purposes in the early 7-series, the carbureted 4.5-liter V-12 would have had only about 3,400 pounds of weight to move around. With a very favorable power-to-weight ratio, and with the smoothness conferred by twelve very small combustion chambers, the resulting prototypes must have been truly exceptional.

In the end, they may have not been exceptional enough: the factory decided that the additional costs associated with building (and running) the cars could not be justified. A simpler way of extracting more power for the 7-series was sought.

THE 745i

Even though a 12-cylinder E-23 7-series would have been magnificent, the compromise offered by the company was still cause for excitement. The production 745i used a *turbocharged* version of BMW's well-proven inline 6-cylinder engine. While turbocharging production engines for higher performance had become relatively popular by the early-1980s, the factory's approach was set-apart by their typical engineering thoroughness and attention to detail.

BMW heralded the arrival of their new executive performance car with the announcement, "The BMW 745i: A progressive technology that opens up new perspectives for top-of-the-range luxury saloons." The company's literature went on to say that

"The days of conventional performance provided by engines of exaggerated size are certainly over. The 745i, therefore, is an impressive example of how you can satisfy the highest demands in terms of performance, safety, economy, comfort and luxury with an engine of reasonable size. It proves that a luxury car can meet the tougher requirements of the future. And this exceptional quality puts the BMW 745i in a future-oriented class of its own that stands out distinctly from conventional automobiles. With the 745i, BMW presents a most advanced concept in the exclusive range of outstanding saloons." Here, BMW presented their turbocharged alternative to the 12-cylinder engine as a better solution— although it seems likely that few would have found much to complain about if the larger motor had gone into production.

The first-series 745i (built from 1981 to 1983) utilized the turbocharged 3210cc engine commonly referred to as the 3.3-liter. That installation produced 252bhp, and provided a significant increase in performance (relative to the automatic-equipped versions of the 733i and 735i). Later cars (from 1984 to 1986) incorporated essentially the same components attached to the company's 3.5-liter engine. The latter car also incorporated an air-to-air intercooler. The other important difference between the two is in their transmissions; as with the rest of the 7-series, early cars made due with the 3-speed automatic while the later version used the more sophisticated (and electronically adjustable) 4-speed auto-

A later E-23 745i. With a turbocharged 3.5-liter engine, the later 745is combined excellent accommodation and comfort with very strong performance.

matic. While the factory listed horsepower as unchanged between the two versions of the 745i, torque was significantly improved in the later cars. Second-generation 745is are capable of accelerating from 0-100 kilometers per hour in about 7.9 seconds, and have a top speed of approximately 228 kilometers per hour.

Both Alpina and Korman (in the U.S.) offered upgrade kits for the later (3.5-liter) 745i. Those packages allowed for greater turbo boost pressures, and raised horsepower to in excess of 300bhp.

A very few 745is were apparently built with the ZF 5-speed manual transmission. These cars are estimated to number approximately 12, but several others have been converted to that transmission (a not too difficult procedure).

Both the 3.2 and 3.5-liter versions of the 745i were highly popular with American grey market importers. As such, the cars are today among the most widely-available special high-performance BMWs in the U.S. (together with the early 635CSi and the early M6).

THE 745i: DRIVING IMPRESSIONS

My own experiences with the 3.2-liter 745i, while providing insight into the product, have generally failed to live up to expectations. The combination of relatively high weight, automatic transmission and the low compression ratio necessary for turbocharged applications, leaves the earlier car at something of a disadvantage unless driven very hard (at the highest portion of its engine's operating range). With a curb weight of approximately 3,500 pounds, the 3-speed automatic transmission and a turbocharger which only becomes active at higher rpms, the impression is understandable. That opinion should not, however, serve to diminish the importance of the original 745i. Even the earliest examples would be entirely worthwhile daily transportation—offering a higher level of equipment and performance than any other (same-year) 7-series.

The 3.5-liter 745i solved most of the problems associated with the earlier version. Even so, driven sedately, the car is in many ways indistinguishable from its lesser 735i sibling. While the example with which I am most familiar is lavishly trimmed in water buffalo hide, there is little else to cosmetically differentiate the car from a standard 735i of the same period. Although the 745i possesses a

tighter, more heavily-damped suspension, the difference is not so great as to be immediately apparent. The car's reason d'etre, its 252 horsepower turbocharged engine, stays similarly muted under most normal driving (this characteristic is magnified by the automatic transmission fitted to almost all examples). However, when driven aggressively (and provoked into the higher area of its operating range), the engine takes on a different, more assertive nature, growing louder and notably more forceful. At higher rpms, the 745i is indeed a very fast car, and probably more usable than the earlier version.

A second-series 745i would represent a compelling purchase—the cars are essentially as practical as any of the lesser 7-series, and far more interesting to own and to drive. In the early to mid-1980s, 745is were widely considered the ultimate sedan in Europe. In the U.S., grey-market versions enjoyed considerable success; the car's reputation no doubt contributed to BMW North America's performance reputation (despite their dissatisfaction with the grey market as a whole). While the 745i's performance is in keeping with its reputation, the car should also be seen in context. The factory intended their ultimate 7-series to be an autobahn-fast executive sedan, rather then a four-door race car for the street. Such a car *was* available (at least in the U.K.), but it required a visit to Alpina.

THE ALPINA 7-SERIES B10

With strong growth in the sports sedan market, BMW found the opportunity (and the necessity) to expand their range of products. As such, the E-3 range (including the 2500-3.0Si) was effectively replaced by two different cars. The lower end of the line (the Bavaria in the U.S.) was succeeded by the 5-series, while the 7-series formally replaced the company's top-of-the-line sedan, the 3.0Si.

From a product positioning standpoint, the 7-series was aimed directly at the company's most important rival, Mercedes-Benz. As usual, the driving experience was wholly different from that provided by the competing Mercedes product.

Given the company's focus, it is understandable that Alpina's efforts have historically been given over to the more sporting end of BMW's product range. That said, there has always been a small but enthusiastic market for a large sedan with the performance and handling of a smaller and lighter car. Just as the company built a handful of cars based upon BMW's top-of-the-line 3.0Si sedan (mentioned previously), Alpina also found a small but enthusiastic market for cars built on BMW's popular 7-series. This time, however, the cars were conceived and built outside of Germany; Synter, Alpina's U.K. authorized distributor was responsible for the E-23 B10.

Alpina's decision *not* to build a version of the 7-series outside of the U.K. was likely influenced by the existence of the 745i. It would have been difficult to significantly improve upon that very capable car (especially in its later series-two form). For 745i owners desiring still more power, Alpina did offer a turbocharger upgrade package allowing higher levels of boost.

The 745i was, however, never available within the U.K. market. Due to the placement of that car's turbocharger, the 745i was never produced in a right-hand-drive model. (It is worth noting that similar packaging issues have historically deprived the U.K. and other right-hand-drive markets of Alpina's turbocharged models). For Synter, the decision to produce and market a naturally-spirated Alpina 7-series must have been an easy one.

If the 735i B10 was conceived in Great Britain, it was nonetheless an Alpina in every respect. As with the rest of the company's B10 U.K.-assembled range (including the 5-series and 6-series), hand-built 260bhp Alpina engines were delivered fully built from Germany to Synter. As with the engine, the rest of the car was pure Alpina; included in the

BMW's second-generation 7-series—the long-wheelbase, 12-cylinder 750iL.

Even with a curb weight of 4,200 pounds, the top of the line 7-series is capable of 0-60 miles per hour acceleration in 7.0 seconds.

package were special gas-filled Bilstein shock absorbers and progressive rate spring, 16-inch Alpina alloys, Alpina front and rear spoilers (the latter an especially attractive piece) and all of the other smaller bits and pieces which distinguished the company's cars.

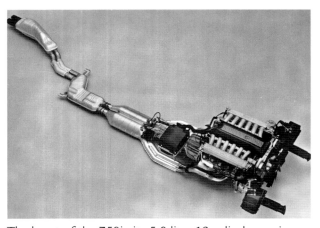

The heart of the 750i—its 5.0 liter 12-cylinder engine.

Capable of 0-60 miles per hour in 6.8 seconds, and with a top speed of approximately 145 miles per hour, the 735i B10 was not just a substitute for the 745i, it was actually superior to it. That superiority derived not only from the car's performance capability, but also from the way that performance could be realized. Without the limitations of either an automatic transmission (as fitted to almost every 745i) or turbo lag, the Alpina car was both faster and more enjoyable to drive than the turbocharged car. This ability, however, came at a substantial price; as tested by a U.K. magazine in April 1985, the 735i B10 was priced at just over (U.K. Pounds) 33,000.

For BMW and Alpina enthusiasts in the U.K., the 735i B10 must represent an attractive purchase on the used market. While finding one of the few cars produced may not be easy (Synter may be able to help), the search would almost certainly be worthwhile.

OTHER EFFORTS:
THE SOUTH AFRICAN 745i

BMW's South African operations have at times produced some of the more compelling derivations of the company's model range. While that subsidiary builds cars which are generally identical in specification to those produced by BMW A.G., there have been certain exceptions.

For the ultimate 7-Series, BMW S.A. spared no effort; their car was both unique and probably the best of its kind. Where BMW in Germany resorted to turbocharging to achieve extraordinary power levels for the 7-Series, BMW South Africa went for a simpler (though probably more expensive) solution. The 745i for that market incorporated the Motorsport 24-valve 3.5-Liter 6-Cylinder engine from the M635CSi (later renamed the M6). The combination of the Motorsport engine with BMW's large sedan proved to be a successful one, with the 745i delighting those fortunate enough to experience it.

It is not known if any South African-specification 745is exist outside of that country. All are right-hand-drive.

THE SECOND-GENERATION
(E-32) 7-SERIES

By the mid-1980s, manufacturers of expensive cars were responding to the demands of their cus-

While this 5.0 liter engine was originally planned for the first-generation 7-series, it did not make it into production until very much later.

tomers for ever larger and more luxurious vehicles. As a result, the luxury sedan segment of the market began to comprise cars which were certainly larger than they needed to be, and which sacrificed qualities such as maneuverability, efficiency and driving enjoyment. BMW's response to the demands of that market was their second-generation (E-32) 7-series—a range of cars which met the requirements of the market while remaining true to BMW's heritage.

The company initially produced two separate models of the new 7-series; a six-cylinder model based on their existing engine range, and the 750i which accommodated BMW's entirely new 5.0-liter 12-cylinder engine. Introduced in 1986, that model (in both standard-wheelbase form and as the 750iL with an additional 4 inches in length) significantly advanced the state-of-the-art for performance luxury sedans. Despite a curb weight of almost 4,200 pounds (U.S. specifications), the 750iL offered 0-60 miles per hour acceleration of 7.0 seconds and an (electronically-limited) top speed of 155 miles per

The Alpina B12 5.0. Based on BMW's 750i, the Alpina version raised horsepower to 350bhp, and provided acceleration from 0-100 kilometers per hour in only 6.9 seconds. The B12 was fitted with numerous modifications to its suspension and braking systems to handle the additional power.

hour. While those performance figures are impressive, the ease with which they are obtained is truly remarkable. With almost unmatched refinement and apparently limitless reserves of power and

117

The company's B11 4.0 (based on the 740i) and B12 5.0 (based on the 750i) offer significant performance improvement over the standard models. The B12 5.0 is capable of a top speed of approximately 172 miles per hour. *Alpina Automobile Meisterwerke catalog*

Although there was relatively little demand for specially-tuned versions of BMW's first-generation 7-series, Alpina now provides a wide range of products for the most recent version of that car. *Automobile Meisterwerke catalog*

BMW's E-38 7-series with Alpina equipment, including the company's special 20-inch alloy wheels.

torque, the 12-cylinder engine feels at times as smooth and flexible as an electric motor.

THE ALPINA B12 5.0 7-Series

Almost immediately following BMW's introduction of their larger and more 'upmarket' 7-series, Alpina offered a more sporting alternative to the standard product. Starting with the short-wheelbase 750i, Alpina modified or augmented nearly every critical component on that car. Beginning with the power plant, Alpina's technicians proved fully up to the task of modifying the new (and hugely complex) 12-cylinder engine. Although the standard displacement was retained,

Alpina's proprietary tuning program extracted 350bhp from the engine—allowing 0-100 kilometers per hour acceleration to be achieved in only 6.9 seconds. With 50 additional horsepower (and with the elimination of BMW's speed-limiting electronics), the B12 5.0 is capable of a top speed of over 172 miles per hour.

As usual, Alpina's efforts were not limited to engine tuning. Their largest-ever sedan also featured a complete rework of the suspension, with special springs, custom-valved Bilstein gas pressure shock absorbers, special suspension mounts and bushings and their own light-alloy wheels (8.5x17-inch front, 9.5x17-inch rear).

CHAPTER 10

The 8-Series Cars

The 8-series coupe represented BMW's replacement for their enormously successful (and long-running) 6-series. At its introduction, it was immediately apparent that the new 8-series represented a considerable break from company tradition. The 850i was neither lighter nor more agile than its competition. Unlike previous efforts, the 8-series was far more a showcase for advanced technology than an everyday car for enthusiastic drivers. While BMW's magnificent 5.0-liter engine (as used in the 750i/iL) endowed the car with exceptional performance, the 850i was both very heavy (at about 4,000 pounds) and probably larger than it needed to be. With that sort of size and weight, the car's abilities were not nearly as accessible as cars such as the M6, or even the 635CSi. Additionally, at a price of about $100,000 upon introduction, 850is were not typically purchased by customers eager to explore the cars' ultimate capabilities.

If the 850i has been something of a disappointment both to enthusiasts and to BMW themselves, it nonetheless provided owners with a wholly satisfactory alternative to cars such as the large Mercedes coupe and the Porsche 928 S4. The comparison to the largest Porsche is interesting, as the 6-series had been current during much of that car's life. The 635CSi had been criticized (more in Europe than in the U.S.) for lacking

The 850CSi, BMW's answer to those who believed that the standard 850i lacked sufficient power.

Various views of the 850i, BMW's replacement for their long-running 6-series coupe.

The 850i engine—with 300bhp and wonderful flexibility. It is identical to the powerplant fitted to the 750iL.

While BMW's magnificent 5.0-liter engine (as used in the 750i/iL) endowed the car with exceptional performance, the 850i was both very heavy (at about 4,000 pounds) and probably larger than it needed to be.

some measure of the 928's power and speed. While the M635CSi/M6 redressed the balance of power between the two companies' flagship models, the critical acclaim garnered by the 928 must have had some significant influence of the development of the 850i. The other logical competitor—the large Mercedes coupe—would also have been very much in the minds of the designers of the 850i. With European luxury cars becoming larger, heavier and more expensive (primarily in an effort to avoid direct competition with Japanese manufacturers as they moved their products up market), the size and weight of the 850i was perhaps unavoidable. Thankfully, that trend seems to have now peaked, with both BMW and

Mercedes focusing on creating exceptional coupes and sports sedans with more moderate proportions (witness the recent successes of BMW's second-generation M3 and the Mercedes/AMG C36).

The 8-series range was substantially overhauled in 1995 with the introduction of both the 840i and the 850CSi. While the 840i was intended as a lower-price alternative using the company's 4.0-liter V-8 engine, the 850CSi (see below) was positioned to compete at the highest-end of the sports/luxury market.

The Alpina 8-Series Cars

For those for whom their 850i was either not fast enough or, more likely, not very much fun to drive, there were alternatives from the usual sources. The 8-series provided Alpina with the basis for a true supercar (both in terms of speed and price).

Alpina's B12 5.0 Coupe represented a similar conversion to the company's B12 5.0 7-series sedan (mentioned previously). With 50 additional horsepower, the Alpina-modified coupe was certainly faster; 0-100 kilometers per hour acceleration was now achieved in 6.8 seconds, with the car achieving a top speed of over 175 miles per hour. As with Alpina's B12 7-series, the B12 5.0 Coupe was a completely upgraded car, with numerous upgrades including a fully modified and higher-specification suspension system.

While Alpina's B12 5.0 Coupe would likely have met the needs of nearly every 8-series enthusiast, Alpina's flagship for the mid-1990s repre-

Substantially larger, heavier and more expensive than the outgoing 6-series, the 850i generated considerable controversy when introduced. Despite its bulk, the 8-series was capable of impressive performance.

sented an even more impressive effort. For their B12 5.7 Coupe, Alpina increased the capacity of this, the largest of all BMW engines, still further—to 5.7-liters. By increasing both the bore and stroke of the 12-cylinder engine (now at 86mm and 81mm, respectively), Alpina achieved a capacity of 5646cc. With compression now at 10.0:1, and with numerous other modifications and upgrades, this new engine produced enormous power—fully 416bhp at 5400rpm.

While the 8-series bodywork was left essentially alone (with the exception of an Alpina front spoiler identical to that fitted to the B12 5.0, Alpina's B12 5.7 was provided with a specially developed carbon fiber hood with ventilation slots and an NACA inlet. Those openings provide additional cooling to the enlarged engine, and the change from steel to carbon fiber must have reduced the weight over the front wheels by a bit.

Not surprisingly, the B12 5.7 Coupe provided shattering performance; 0-100 kilometers per hour acceleration is achieved in only 5.8 seconds, with the car able to produce a top speed of 186 miles per hour. Equally remarkable was the price; at DM 233,478 in 1994, it is doubtful that more than a handful of Alpina's 5.7-liter Coupes were produced.

THE HARTAGE 8-SERIES CARS

With the development of their own more powerful 8-series, Hartage continued to provide an interesting alternative to Alpina's conversions. The Hartage H8-6.0 engine conversion for the 850i/CSi included the fitting of that company's own pistons and crankshaft, moving displacement up to a full 6.0 liters (5992cc). With that increased displacement, and with additional Hartage tuning (including the reworking of the engine's, the H8 provided 430bhp and massive (610 Nm) torque. So configured, the H8 was apparently good for 0-100 kilometers per hour acceleration in 5.5 seconds. Top speed is unlisted, but must have been something above 175 miles per hour.

The 850i interior, luxuriously outfitted with almost every possible extra.

THE BMW M8

Although destined to remain a one-off, the M8 provided BMW with the perfect answer to those who failed to appreciate their 8-series coupe. The M8 was essentially an enthusiast's ideal version of the 850i; both significantly lighter and more powerful than the standard car, the M8 was built by the Motorsport Division with the goal of moving it into limited production. The Motorsport program began with the engine; in place of the standard unit was a 6.0-liter, 4-valve per cylinder power plant producing approximately 550bhp. Extensive use of carbon fiber and lightweight plastics substantially reduced the car's weight. Unfortunately, the M8's unveiling came at a time when large, ultra high-performance cars were (and continue to be) politically unpopular. While there is doubtless merit in the argument that such cars consume far more than their fair share of the planet's natural resources, it is also unlikely that anyone actually *uses* such cars to any great extent.

In any case, the M8 remains an unfinished project—never produced, but almost certainly the most desirable BMW coupe of the 1990s.

The 850CSi

While the Motorsport Division was unable to move the M8 into production, the company did offer a somewhat more conservative version for those looking for greater performance from the 8-series. While the 850CSi failed to remove any weight from BMW's largest-ever coupe, that car was equipped with even more horsepower and better handling then the original 850i. For the factory's ultimate production 8-series, the Motorsport Division enlarged the 5.0-liter 12-cylinder engine to 5.6-liters (5576cc), and raised compression from 8.8:1 to 9.8:1. So configured, the 850CSi produced 372 horsepower (50bhp over the standard 850i), and 402 foot-pounds of torque. Revised suspension components (providing a 10mm lower ride height) enabled BMW's top 8-series to make use of its additional power. A Getrag 6-speed gearbox, a special spoiler package and 17-inch forged alloy wheels completed the package. Despite a curb weight of over 4,200 pounds, the 850CSi was fully as fast as its M6 predecessor, sprinting from 0-60 miles per hour in just 5.7 seconds. As with all recent German high performance cars, top speed is electronically limited to 155 miles per hour.

Alpina's B12 5.0 Coupe. Based on the 850Ci, Alpina's work raised the B12 5.0's power to 350bhp. *Alpina Automobile Meisterwerke catalog*

Alpina's masterwork—the B12 5.7 engine. The 476bhp provided by this engine endows even the very heavy 8-series coupe with extremely strong performance.

The ultimate Alpina, at least at the time of this writing. The B12 5.7 probably comes closer to replicating the performance of BMW's one-off M8 than anything else. With engine displacement expanded to 5646cc, and with the benefit of Alpina's extensive tuning work, the B12 5.7 provides 416bhp. The car is extensively modified in almost every respect, and is capable of a top speed of approximately 186 miles per hour. *Alpina Automobile Meisterwerke catalog*

With an additional 50bhp (now up to 372bhp), and with a completely reworked suspension system, the 850CSi was significantly faster and better-handling than the standard car. Acceleration from 0-60 miles per hour could now be achieved in only 5.7 seconds.

CHAPTER 11

Epilogue

BMW's reputation as a builder of high-quality, high-performance automobiles is secure; during the postwar period, the company has created some of the most interesting and useful cars made.

That said, BMW's postwar efforts can be divided into two separate categories: the high-volume production which is the basis of the company's business, and the more specialized work which has helped to secured BMW's image as a builder of performance vehicles. We have here been concerned with the latter category; the cars which have helped to create and sustain BMW's worldwide reputation.

Someone not familiar with BMW's history and the intricacies of their models designations (as most are not), nonetheless probably regard BMWs as high-performance cars. That same person, if testing a BMW when shopping for a new car, may or may not come away impressed with the performance of the car. The point is that while all BMWs are well-engineered automobiles built to admirable standards, some BMWs were designed to be truly extraordinary devices. We hope that this work does credit to the quality of those machines.

This 1987 M3 Evolution was photographed just outside of Munich, Germany in the rural countryside. The car is owned by BMW Mobile Tradition. *David Gooley*

Index

Alpina, 16-22, 32, 34, 36, 39, 43, 63, 71, 80, 81, 108

Bovensipen, Burkhard, 16, 17, 19

Callaway Turbosystems, 24, 26

Dietel Enterprises, 82
DINAN Performance Engineering, 26

Hack, Gert, 17
Hartage, 22, 23, 71, 74, 82, 90, 123

Korman Autoworks, 27
Kugelfischer, 34

Models:
    3.0CS, 43
    3.0CSi, 44, 47
    3.0CSL, 42, 45-47, 61, 93, 108
    3.0Si, 42, 93
    300 SEL 6.3, 42
    320i, 77, 78
    320iS, 88
    323i Turbo, 91
    323i, 82
    325i, 90
    333i, 85, 86, 88
    345i, 82
    528 B6, 63
    528i, 58, 59, 64
    533i, 58, 59
    633 CSi, 108
    635CSi, 60, 61,66, 105, 121
    733i, 111, 113
    735i, 112, 113, 115
    745i, 113, 114, 115, 116
    750i, 116, 117, 121
    750iL, 116, 121
    850CSi, 124
    850i, 121
    1600, 32-34
    1800Ti, 29, 31
    1800TiSA, 29, 30
    2000CS, 31, 32, 43, 93

2000Ti, 31
2000Tii, 31
2000TILux, 31
2002, 33-39, 41, 52, 57, 77-79
2002tii, 34, 44
2800CS Coupe, 35
2800CS, 32, 43
B7, 63
B10 Biturbo, 73
B10, 109, 115
B12, 117, 122, 123
B3 3.0, 99
B6, 19, 20, 22, 80, 81
B7 Turbo, 71, 108
B7, 20, 21, 64, 65, 109
B9, 109
Batmobile, 46
C1, 89
CLS II, 100
E-12, 57-59, 61-65, 103
E-21, 78, 80-82
E-28, 71, 72
E-3, 41
E-9, 43, 103
E028, 70, 71
H35, 90
H8, 123
M3, 37, 82-84, 88, 89, 93, 94, 97, 98
M1, 20, 49, 51, 52, 59, 62
M3L, 98
M49, 59
M5, 20, 66, 68-72, 74, 97
M535i, 59, 60-62, 65-67, 71
M6, 27, 90, 93, 97, 105, 106, 109, 122, 124
M635 CSi, 167, 06
M8, 124
S3 Sport 2.5, 91-93
S3 Sport CSL, 99, 100
S5, 71
Z1, 22

Schnitzer, AC, 23, 24, 37, 71, 82, 91, 92, 99, 100
Sieff, 58